KNITTING
IN THE
OLD WAY

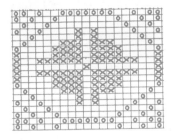

Priscilla A. Gibson-Roberts
photography by John VanSant Roberts

In honor of the knitters of yesteryear who, amid much hardship, created a rich legacy of patterns and designs for those who follow.

ISBN 0-934026-20-3
Library of Congress Catalog Number 85-081330

5M:985:JLP/VC

 INTERWEAVE PRESS
306 North Washington Avenue
Loveland, Colorado 80537

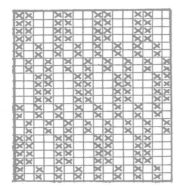

CONTENTS

Author's Note

In writing this book, I've assumed that we share a reasonable amount of experience: that you know the basic knitting stitches, that you've knit a few sweaters on your own. I strongly recommend that you read the book through, because the techniques described build on each other. If you try to use one part without having read what came before, you'll probably feel frustrated.

The last chapter, on handspinning, is one that you won't find in most knitting books, but is of special interest to me. Sheila McGregor, an authority on traditional knitting, has found from studying museum collections throughout Europe that there was as much variation in the knitting yarns of the 18th and 19th centuries as there is today. The methods I present are not the only ones for preparing good knitting yarns, but they have proven themselves for me in use.

I've made every effort to accurately portray the history of the traditional folk sweaters that I so dearly love. But because there are so many conflicting theories about their origins, antiquity, and materials, I've included only that information that seems to be based on sound research and common sense. New information may outdate my conclusions in time.

Much of my research has been based on written descriptions, drawings, and old photographs rather than on first-hand inspection of actual garments. Therefore, I haven't attempted to reproduce the patterns or designs of particular old sweaters; rather, I've presented composites that capture the essence of each style.

In both my spinning and knitting, I've tried to place myself in the frame of mind of a knitter of those earlier times, always aware of the demands life placed her time and physical strength. As a result, my admiration of the handspinners and handknitters of bygone eras is boundless!

Priscilla A. Gibson-Roberts

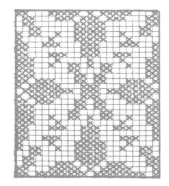

Introduction

Events of the 20th century—the World Wars, revival of the Olympic Games, migrations of peoples, and increased world trade—have all played their part in bringing the folk knitting of many cultures to the world at large. The study of sweaters from other cultures and times has accelerated in the past decade with more and more handknitters seeking to express themselves through historically interesting garments rather than the fashions of the moment. Masterfully handcrafted sweaters of other countries show us, though, that knitting skills have been badly neglected for generations in the industrialized nations, most especially in the United States. Printed patterns and lengthy written instructions have replaced intuitive design skills and a thorough understanding of technique. A once simple and delightful craft has become shrouded in elaborate line-by-line instructions, enough to daunt the most skillful knitter while thoroughly intimidating the novice. But, armed with a general overview of sweater construction and some basic sweater formulas, today's knitter can once again be in control of the craft, knitting in the old way.

It's only a short step back to the era of beautiful folk sweaters, for sweaters as we know them today date back no earlier than the 17th century and are largely the product of the 19th century. True, many garments were made from knitted fabric prior to sweaters: the fabric was knit in the round, felted, cut, and tailored into jackets and trousers. But sweaters themselves most likely evolved from undergarments, and as they came out from 'under', they became glorious expressions of their respective cultures.

Most knitters today are familiar with sweaters whose roots lie in traditional folk knitting. There are for example, the Guernsey (or Gansey) with its knit-purl designs and simple cables covering the chest and upper arms; the Fair Isle with its bands of designs in ever-changing color combinations; the Aran with its bold embossed texture of intricate cables, bobbles and interlaced stitches; the classic Nordic with its color stranded stars and flecks; the Icelandic yoke in the natural colors of luxurious Icelandic wool. But what of their history and the many variations within these general styles? And what of the lesser known styles? The Bavarian with its intricate criss-crossing of travel ing twisted stitches on a purl ground; the Tyrolean sprinkled with gay embroidered alpine flowers; the elaborate Hebridean with panels of varied designs; the Swedish Bohus with its subtle color shadings and textures on delicately designed yokes; the Danish brocade blouse patterned after damask weaving; the red and black lumberjack sweaters of Sweden; the robust Cowichan Indian sweaters of Canada. Part of the excitement of folk knitting is the realization that unique styles evolved in many small pockets of the world—and that more are waiting to be discovered!

Today's knitters are often interested in going beyond recreating a folk sweater in modern yarns. They want to use traditional-style yarns, but there appears to be little information available on the types of yarns used in traditional sweaters much less on how to select the best and most appropriate from the many styles and brands available today. For many, interest in folk knitting coincides with a revived interest in handspinning—and how better to express one's creativity and ingenuity than with a handspun yarn knit up into an authentic folk sweater? But, once again, there has been a gap in passing this basic knowledge from one generation to another—a serious gap, as there are many techniques for spinning knitting yarns, with some more suitable than others for specific sweater styles.

This book is an effort to help today's handknitters select or spin their yarns and identify and adapt the various folk designs and construction techniques which have served so well for so long in traditional knitting around the world. Bear in mind these techniques were passed from one generation to the next by word of mouth, aided only by simple graphs and samplers; therefore, it was not unusual for many styles or variations on a style to evolve, their actual origins lost in time. Traditions change; new ways develop and become incorporated into the old, making handknitting (and for that matter, handspinning) a dynamic craft. Without clinging to the past just for the sake of tradition, we must preserve what is good, adapting it to meet today's needs.

In the melting pot culture in which we live today, we can cross cultural lines and draw on all the old ways, often using modern adaptations of old techniques. I hope this book will help both knitters and the spinners to create freely from the many styles and designs of knitted folk sweaters, returning to the old way of simply understanding what to do rather than duplicating designs from printed patterns. This path can lead us to self-expression through unique, one-of-a-kind creations of enduring quality.

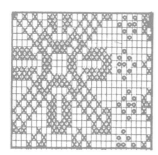
Origins

Knitting is a venerable craft, but it is young compared to spinning and weaving. In fact, most textile historians now believe that it is the youngest of all the basic textile techniques. Although historians had dated the earliest knitted fragment to about A.D. 200, recent detailed studies indicate this piece resulted from another textile construction which creates a knit-like fabric by interlooping yarn with an eyed needle.

Mary Thomas, in her classic *Knitting Book*, describes in detail a crossed-stitch knitting technique said to have been used in an early fragment, but subsequent research has indicated the piece was actually made by a single needle technique of interlooping short strands of loosely twisted yarn. This technique, in various forms, was practiced in many parts of the world, with magnificent examples coming from the highly skilled workers of both Peru and Northern Europe. Even today, *nalbindning*, a similar technique, is practiced in some Scandinavian countries. In addition, knotless netting, sprang and even embroidery can look enough like knitting to confuse even the most expert textile scholars.

Knitting as it is understood today, and as I will use the term in this book, is a technique in which a single continuous strand of yarn is worked into rows of interlocking loops on a set of two or more needles which are pointed at one or both ends. The earliest example of this kind of knitting, patterned cotton socks found in Egypt, dates back to only A.D. 1100.

Knitting is currently believed to have developed with the Arabian nomad, who, in turn, carried it into Egypt. Knowledge of the craft apparently spread from there across North Africa and into Spain, from whence it was introduced throughout Europe under the auspices of the Roman Catholic church. While this is the current line of thought, there are still some riddles: items from India that appear to have been knitted prior to the 11th century, and a set of bone needles found in the south of France, possibly knitting tools, dating from the 2nd century. Obviously, there is room for more research.

Regardless of where or when it started, knitting swept across the European continent relatively quickly. During Medieval times knitted garments became highly prized, with silk gloves and stockings a prerogative of the rich. Professional guilds controlled the market, and knitted garments became the fashion of the wealthy class. Demand became so great that knitting became a cottage industry, with the peasantry subsidizing their meager livelihoods by knitting woolen caps and socks for the gentry. Thus the craft passed into the hands of women who began to incorporate knitting into the attire of their own families, possibly as early as the 15th century.

By the early 18th century, handknitting was practiced throughout the civilized world by entire populations, young and old, male and female, in widely diverse cultures. But at the very peak of its popularity, the decline of knitting was foretold by the coming Industrial Revolution. By 1589, a knitting-frame had been invented by William Lee of Cambridge, England. As is often the case, the new and the old lived side by side through many generations, but eventually handknitting as a significant cottage industry all but collapsed. Knitting continued in the home, and became elevated to a feminine parlor art during Victorian times; this ushered in the era of written instructions for elegant young ladies who didn't have the benefit of passed-down samplers and charts which had served the common folk so well for so long. Fashion garments, rather than the craft itself, became the focal point; flat knitting replaced the natural and efficient circular techniques used for generations.

At the same time, though, in some rural areas, people kept to the old ways. Here, handknits were a part of everyday wear, and knitting itself remained a minor cottage industry. In these more isolated areas with cultures less affected by external influences, unique designs and techniques were perfected. This does not mean that new ideas were not introduced, only that the old, proven ways were not discarded. During this period, it was discovered that knitting made excellent woolen 'shirts'. These were probably worn initially as undergarments. The oldest fragment known to have been part of such a garment is a sleeve found in Denmark, dating back to the 17th century. Although records indicate that vests and shirtlike garments were knit as early as the 14th century, this fragment is the first indication of a knitted woolen garment designed for use as outerwear—quite possibly the forerunner of the modern sweater. Since knitted garments, particularly those of the peasantry, were used, worn out and discarded or recycled, little is known of these early predecessors of traditional folk sweaters.

When did the sweater as we know it today first appear? And where? Possibly in the late 17th century, but certainly by the beginning of the 19th century, the sweater—often called a jersey or jumper, and sometimes referred to as a knitted frock in historic records—seems to have spontaneously appeared in many isolated cultures in the northern climes: the British Isles, Scandinavia, eastern Europe. The oldest example is possibly the *natrøje*, a damask brocade blouse of Denmark. The undergarment of little distinction seems to have been transformed into a glorious expression of creativity, and a new era in knitted folkwear was born.

Aside from all the myths and tales surrounding folk sweaters, this is a craft that has probably developed in only the last two or three hundred years! And yet, it is in these garments that the most charming aspects of knitting have been expressed: ingenuity, spontaneity and creativity, functionalism and regional style.

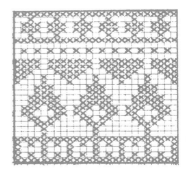

Traditional Yarns

Fiber content

Knitting yarns can be spun from wool, silk, flax, cotton, hair, and a legion of synthetic fibers, but yarns for traditional folk sweaters were almost always wool. Sometimes, other fibers such as mohair or silk were blended with it, but wool was the major component of the yarn. Silk was much too expensive for common folk (though it was used in knitted garments for the nobility in early times). Cotton needs a warm climate with a long growing season, making it unavailable to many cultures. Flax, being inelastic, has never lent itself well to knitting. Last, and most obvious, synthetic fibers are inventions of the 20th century, so they had no place in traditional folkwear.

The intrinsic properties of the wool fiber should class it as a miracle fiber, possibly the most functional of all fibers available to mankind. Wool can absorb up to 30% of its weight in moisture without feeling wet; and when wet, it actually generates a minute amount of heat which offsets any clamminess that might result from excess dampness. This property made it invaluable for fishermen and farm workers who were often out in cold, wet weather. Wool is highly elastic, a property which can be enhanced in the spinning, allowing a garment to give and yet return to its original shape time and time again. It is soil resistent, and if properly finished, washable. Almost all wool knitting yarns available today are hand washable, and many are machine washable, making the handknit garment easy-care with only minimal precautions. Wool is water repellant, a property which can be enhanced if some natural oils are retained in the processing or if the wool is oiled after processing. It is an excellent insulator, used by desert nomads to keep the heat out and by arctic dwellers to keep the heat in. Wool is a renewable resource, available throughout the world and not overly expensive. A well-made wool yarn properly constructed into a fabric and garment will wear well while retaining its good looks year in and year out.

Wool does have some negative properties, though with proper handling these can be minimized or even turned to advantage. Take felting, for example. In the presence of heat, moisture and pressure or agitation, wool fibers will mat together, interlocking to form a solid mass. (Did you ever accidentally put a sweater through the washer and dryer on hot?) This is how felt fabric is made, and early woolen knitwear was often felted deliberately to make it more wind and water resistant. Felting can be disastrous if the process is triggered accidentally, but care in handling virtually eliminates the danger. When washing, don't agitate the wool; allow it to soak clean. Don't place wool directly into hot water—it can actually be boiled without matting or shrinking *if* the process begins in warm water and the temperature is raised to the boiling point very gradually, and then gradually allowed to cool. What must be avoided is shocking the wool with either extremely hot or cold temperatures. Don't wring out the moisture; gently squeeze it out. After you've squeezed the excess moisture out, the fibers, yarn, fabric or garment can be placed in a laundry bag and spun in a washing machine to extract more moisture and speed the drying process. The centrifugal force alone won't result in felting.

Pilling is another problem that arises with some wool yarn, but again, there are ways to deal with it. Pilling is simply the balling up of short, loose fibers on the surface of the fabric. The more loose fibers available, the more likely that pills will develop. Usually, the pills break off as they form; simply picking off the excess will usually control the problem. If pilling is extreme and becomes unsightly, you might want to give the surface a careful shearing with a razor. Your choice of yarn can minimize this problem, for the amount of pilling is directly related to the amount of short, loose surface fibers and noils (very short fibers clumped together) that are free to ball together. A yarn with smooth surface, free from excess fuzz—such as a well-made worsted yarn—will be resistant to pilling. Also, the more firmly spun the yarn and the more uniform the fiber length, the fewer pills it will have. You can check a yarn by drawing it between your fingers repeatedly to see if it tends to fuzz up. Pull out several individual fibers and check their length, too.

One of the most common complaints about wool garments is their scratchiness. Many people claim an allergy to wool—though you'll seldom hear of an allergy to sheep. Yes, wool fibers can be irritating to the skin *if* a harsh and scratchy wool fleece is used in the yarn. But a number of wool breeds—Merino, for example—produce a soft, fine, non-irritating fiber. Actually, much of the skin irritation attributed to wool in the last half century is probably a result of dyes, chemicals and harsh physical treatment during processing, rather than the wool itself. Careful selection of yarn can eliminate this problem. Always test the yarn against a tender spot—neck, cheek or forehead—and not just with your fingertips. Or better yet, turn to handspinning! A yarn made from a carefully selected fleece, lovingly processed with gentle carding that doesn't tear the fibers, and washed with a gentle detergent, will result in a non-irritating yarn which even many allergy-sufferers can't resist.

Yarn Construction and Selection

Two basic spinning systems are used in commercial yarn construction: woolen and worsted. Woolen yarn is made from wool fibers which have been carded from shorter fibers (ranging from about 1″ to 4″), and spun into a light, fluffy, somewhat fuzzy yarn of randomly arranged fibers. Worsted yarn, on the other hand, is made of longer fibers (typically 4″ or more), all about the same length, lying parallel and spun into a strong, smooth, dense yarn.

Mass-produced, commercially spun domestic knitting yarns have tended to be a homogenized lot, made from fibers that haven't been sorted by sheep breed. It is processed in large mixed batches to remove the oils and extraneous vegetable matter with acid baths, harsh mechanical picking, and other harsh chemical and physical processes. For woolen yarns, the fibers are carded by being passed through a system of rollers with wire teeth which straighten them into a thin web. The web is then divided into long narrow strips called slivers (pronounced to rhyme with 'divers'), which in turn are rubbed together to form a roving, the final step before spinning.

Worsted yarns are treated in the same way through the sliver stage. At this point, the sliver is drawn through a combing system to straighten and align the long fibers and remove the shorter ones. These long fibers are then drawn out into a continuous long, smooth 'top' which is then spun. In the spinning process itself, both the woolen roving and the worsted top are drawn through rollers to stretch the fiber mass and reduce it to the specified diameter, then wound onto revolving bobbins which insert twist, thus creating a one ply or 'singles' yarn.

The commercial spinning process is an extension of hand methods which have been done for centuries, but along the way it has become mechanized and standardized so that all fibers are spun in much the same way. The fibers, whether long or short, coarse or fine, are subject to the requirements of the machine, instead of the machine and method being adapted to suit the fiber. A few imported knitting yarns are sorted by breed as well as grade, then spun to enhance their natural character; the lovely Icelandic and Shetland yarns are good examples. Though mass-produced, they are less rigorously handled than many American yarns and so retain their naturally soft, non-irritating 'hand' or feel. (A word of warning: in some countries, 'wool' does not necessarily denote the fiber content, but rather is used interchangeably with the term 'yarn'.) Luckily, with the recent resurgence of interest in textile crafts and especially handknitting, specialty mills in the U.S. are beginning to produce high quality knitting yarns, as demanded by the discriminating consumer.

Careful selection of knitting yarns will enable you to produce a traditional sweater of lasting beauty and quality. The best knitting yarns are spun from fine, soft wools of sheep such as Merino, Columbia, or Corriedale, and they are worth seeking out. They are spun with minimal handling and chemical treatment. Some specialty suppliers are even beginning to identify on their labels the breed from which the yarn is spun. The yarn may be lightly or more firmly spun (handknitting yarns today are seldom tightly spun). The lighter spin is softer and more lofty, but not as hard wearing as more firmly spun yarn. As a general frame of reference, the fine to ultra-fine yarns range from 12 to 16 twists per inch in the ply; medium and heavy yarns have from six to 12 twists per inch; and bulky to very bulky or chunky yarns have two to six twists per inch, measured without tension on the yarn.

You must consider sweater design in choosing a yarn of appropriate spin. For example, a more firmly spun yarn produces a clear definition of stitches that's appropriate for knit-purl pattern designs, while a softly spun yarn fluffs up and closes the interstices between stitches and gives a uniform matt-finish surface that shows off multi-color pattern knitting nicely. On the other hand, a firm, smooth yarn of fine diameter can be used in color stranded work to resemble embroidery. A comfort factor to consider is that a softly spun, slightly fuzzy yarn incorporates a lot of air and will be much warmer than a smooth, compact yarn. However, the smooth, compact yarn will have less tendency to pill. A softly spun bulky yarn works up into a garment with the greatest warmth for its weight, but it won't be very wind resistant.

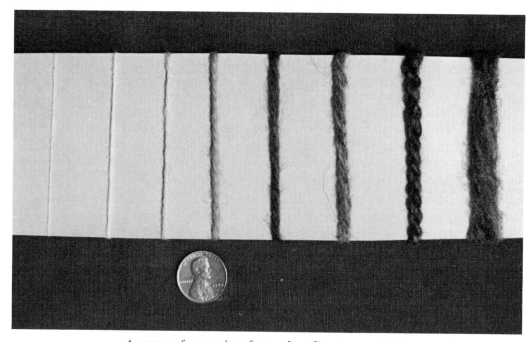

A range of yarn sizes from ultra-fine to very bulky.

Most knitting yarns are plied; that is, they are made of two or more fine strands, or 'singles', twisted together. There is usually very little twist in the individual strands as well as in the plying, so that the yarn is strong and elastic yet lofty.

Selecting between a yarn with two plies or more is largely a matter of personal preference. Although there are exceptions, the structure of a two-ply yarn will usually be more visible on the knit surface than a similar multi-ply yarn, because the individual plies of the two-ply are larger and therefore more visible within the yarn. The multi-ply yarn will be more smoothly rounded with the individual plies less distinctive, and the resulting knit surface smoother both to the hand and eye.

If the yarn has only one ply, choose one with long fibers, a smooth surface and fairly low twist. Short fibers reduce the yarn's strength while increasing its tendency to mat and pill. Be wary of too much twist, too, because if the yarn hasn't been properly blocked by being washed or steamed and dried under tension, your knitted fabric—especially if it's a little loose—will have a decided bias slant.

Highly textured yarns, often called 'novelty' or 'designer' yarns, are a fairly recent development. Plying dissimilar strands together, spinning or plying under variable tension, creating thick and thin, slubby or snarled effects, give unique visual and tactile qualities to yarn. These yarns have opened new avenues in contemporary garment design, but in folk knitting the knitted pattern, not the yarn, is the dominant design feature.

Going beyond yarn structure, you must also consider the impact of color on sweater design. Solid, evenly dyed colors show off pattern knitting best, though the subtle color variations of a heather yarn can be very pleasant, too. Highly variegated color tends to be distracting in both color stranded and embossed textured designs.

Any yarn selection will involve compromise; you'll simply have to think about each project individually, and satisfy its most important needs and sacrifice the lesser.

If you're interested in a more detailed discussion of yarn construction, look at Chapter 10, "Spinning Techniques".

Hands-on Yarn Evaluation

How does knowledge of yarn construction translate into selecting yarn for a given project? The first step is to narrow the field of choice based on the design features of the sweater you're planning, and then judge which yarn best fits all criteria. How even is the yarn along its length? Check the amount of twist: is it high or low, and how does this suit your design needs? Count the plies; if possible, work up a small swatch to see how the plies and level of twist affect the surface appearance. Fray out one of the plies to check the fibers themselves. If the yarn is worsted, the fibers should be long and parallel: if it's woolen, they will be shorter and randomly arranged. A lot of little short fibers and noils foretell a tendency to pill with use. Test for elasticity and resiliency by stretching and releasing; a quality yarn should stretch and return to its original length readily. (A woolen yarn is more elastic than a worsted one.) If in doubt, buy one skein and work with it—it is wiser to spend a few dollars and hours on one skein than to purchase the whole lot and find that it's not suitable for your design.

Yarn Into Fabric

After selecting a yarn appropriate for your sweater design, you need to determine your gauge and how much yarn you'll need. The gauge is the number of stitches in a given measure of fabric, commonly expressed as "stitches per inch". A 4″ (10 cm) measure will give you a more accurate gauge than a 1″ length, especially if you're working with very bulky yarns or handspun yarns that are variable in diameter. The initial consideration in determining gauge is fairly obvious: the larger the yarn diameter, the larger the needle. But beyond diameter, the degree of twist and loft of the yarn must be taken into account. A soft spun yarn is usually knit more loosely to allow the yarn to fill the interstices of the stitches. A more firmly spun yarn is knit in a finer gauge, since there is less available loft to fill in the spaces. Bulky to very bulky yarns are knit loosely to avoid compressing them into a stiff fabric that doesn't show off the character of the yarn. Experience and personal preference are the best guides for coordinationg yarn to needle size.

What we usually look for today in coordinating yarn and needle size is a knit fabric that is slightly firm, smooth and elastic, neither boardlike nor loose and loopy. Historically, though, many of the earliest sweaters were *very* firmly knit of hard spun yarns. There are records of sweaters of such tightly spun, harsh yarn that a scarf around the neck and wrappings on the wrists were needed to protect the skin from abrasion. The first Aran fishing shirt to come to public attention was almost boardlike in its density and stiffness. And some ganseys of fine handspun yarn were so firmly knit that an average man's sweater weighed in excess of 2½ pounds! In the northern European countries, sweaters were often deliberately felted to make them more wind and water resistant. Preferences varied, however, for both the Faroe Islands and Iceland have a longstanding tradition of softly spun woolen yarns. These early garments were, more often than not, fulled (subjected to some shrinking and felting) to make them more comfortable and durable under harsh conditions. Today, we have the same wide latitude of choice, though there are generally accepted standards of durability, comfort and fashion.

How does one go about coordinating all the variables of yarn size, needle size, gauge and yardage requirements? The simplest way is to wrap your yarn around a pencil, dowel or ruler and count the number of wraps per inch; this number can then be used to determine a tentative needle size and gauge, and estimated yardage. A ruler is convenient for counting wraps per inch, as it is already marked in inch intervals, but it's difficult to maintain consistent tension while wrapping around a flat, sharp-edged shape. Wrapping around a pencil or knitting needle is inconvenient, too, because it's hard to hold the yarn in place while you measure it. I've made a special little cylindrical "ruler" just for measuring wraps per inch, and find it very handy. A 6″ length of ¼″ doweling, some time and patience are all you need. Cut a notch about ¼″ deep and ¹⁄₁₆″ wide into the center of one end of your dowels. Sand the dowel and the notch very smoothly so that your

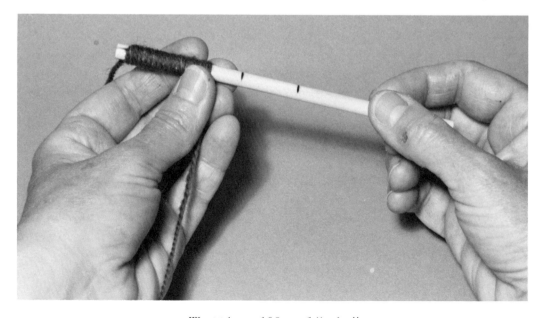

Wrapping a 100 yard "ruler".

yarn can wrap easily without snagging. Mark this "ruler" at 1″ intervals, beginning at the base of the notch; be sure to mark in some way that will not rub off and damage or discolor the yarn. Woodburning works very well, or you can scratch smooth, decisive marks. The ruler will be about the size of a size 10½ knitting needle, convenient for wrapping all yarns.

To use the ruler, catch the end of your yarn in the notch. Tying a knot in the end of finer yarn or fraying out the end of a bulky yarn will help secure it in the notch. Then, laying the notched tip lightly between your thumb and first two fingers, turn the ruler with the other hand to wind the yarn evenly around the ruler. Wrap smoothly, yarn just touching yarn, but *not tightly*; the object is not to pack the yarn onto the ruler. Measure fine yarns over a 1″ interval, medium to heavy yarns over 2″, and bulky to chunky yarns over 3″. When measuring a handspun yarn, you'll get a more meaningful number if you wrap several representative sections and average them.

Then count the number of wraps per inch, and refer to the accompanying chart, "The 100 Yard Rule: Coordinating Yarn to Yardage for a Plain Sweater". The chart is simple to use; each size yarn from ultra-fine at 18 wraps per inch through very bulky at 8 wraps per inch is listed, with corresponding gauge, needle size, and estimated yardage for an average adult sweater (medium, 36″-38″ with 4″ ease).

The 100 Yard Rule
Coordinating Yarn to Yardage for Plain Sweater

Yarn Size: Wraps per Inch	Typical Gauge in Stocking Stitch	Recommended Needle Size	Yardage for Average Adult Sweater (Medium, 36″-38″ plus 2″ ease)
Ultra Fine: 18 or more wraps per inch measured over 1″ (baby to lace weight)	8 or more sts/in (32 or more sts/10cm)	#00-0-1-2 (2mm to 3mm)	1800-2200 yards
Fine: 16 wraps per inch measured over 1″ (fingering weight)	6-8 sts/in (24-32 sts/10cm)	#2-3-4 (3mm to 3¾ mm)	1600-1900 yards
Medium: 14 wraps per inch measured over 2″ (sport weight)	5-6 sts/in (20-24 sts/10cm)	#4-5-6 (3¾ mm to 4½ mm)	1400-1600 yards
Heavy: 12 wraps per inch measured over 2″ (4-ply worsted weight)	4½-5 sts/in (18-20 sts/10cm)	#7-8-9 (5mm to 6mm)	1200-1400 yards
Bulky: 10 wraps per inch measured over 3″	3½-4 sts/in (14-16 sts/10 cm)	#10-10½-11 (6½ mm to 7½ mm)	1000-1200 yards
Very Bulky: 8 or less wraps per inch measured over 3″	2-3 sts/in (8-12 sts/10 cm)	#13-15-16 (9mm to 10mm)	800-1000 yards

The yardage estimate is simply the number of wraps per inch multiplied by 100. In other words, an average adult sweater will require 100 yards for each wrap around the ruler. Obviously, this is only approximate, based on a plain pullover for an average adult. Your actual yardage will vary according to how tightly you wrapped the yarn around the ruler, at what gauge you actually knit, and the design features of both your yarn and the garment itself.

To accommodate a range of sizes, designated below by actual chest measurements, adjust the yardage recommendation as follows:

- Child, 25″ or less: average yardage minus 30%.
- Extra small, 28″-30″: medium yardage minus 20%.
- Small, 32″-34″: medium yardage minus 10%.
- Medium, 36″-38″: 100 yards per wrap.
- Large, 40″-42″: medium yardage plus 10%.
- Extra large, 44″-46″: medium yardage plus 20% or more.

Since all sweaters are not plain pullovers, here are suggested adjustments for some design variables:

- Add up to 10% for greater ease or extra length.
- Subtract about 30% for a sleeveless vest. (The body requires about 60%-70% of the total yardage.)
- Add 10% for heavily textured designs with a high take-in factor.
- Add up to 50% for color stranding. (Reduce the main color when adding other colors; the actual amounts depend on the area covered by the design.)

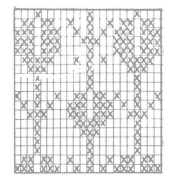

Knitting Techniques

The goal of folk knitters has always been to produce sweaters using the simplest, most efficient means to create the most elaborate designs. Since the knitter of yesteryear was often subsidizing a meager income, speed was important. The industrial knitting frame was supplanting hand knitting, making intricate knitting moves and designs that could not be duplicated on the knitting frame essential. Even in areas where the need for profit did not influence in ethnic designs, the competitive spirit did: many beautiful designs were perfected in response to the intricate work of a fellow knitter.

The simplest way to increase speed and simplify intricate stitches was to knit in the round whenever possible. It's much easier to work a complex pattern with the right side facing you, and you also save a lot of time on finishing tasks, especially the sewing of seams. Not only is elaborate design work simplified with circular knitting, but increases and decreases are easier in a knit stitch than in a purl. Where a flat surface is necessary—between armholes, for instance—you can choose to knit back and forth, or to knit in the round and slash your work. Flat knitted garments with complicated shaping which must be sewn into tubes are the work of commercial yarn producers and designers, not the knitters of old.

Knitting Methods

There are two basic methods in knitting: the English-American style with the yarn carried in the right hand, and the Continental-German system, with the yarn carried in the left. The results of both systems are identical. Each has its advantages: the knit stitch is simpler in the Continental style, while the purl stitch is simpler in the English style. In flat knitting on long unsupported needles which are common today, the Continental method is somewhat less awkward than the English, but the original English method in which a knitting belt supported the needles was very efficient, with speeds up to 200 stitches per minute possible! With circular needles, which need no support, the choice of which system to use is a matter of personal preference. The two methods have lived side by side in Europe for centuries, and among folk knitters, both are often worked within the same garment. If you want to become proficient in ethnic knitting, particularly color stranded designs, you should master both methods.

The English Method. To knit in the English manner, hold the yarn in the right hand, tensioning it on the fingers. My favorite method is to pass it over the first and third fingers, and under the second and fourth, for tensioning. To work a knit stitch, insert the right needle into the bottom of the first stitch on the left needle from front to back, pass the yarn around the point of the right needle from right to left, and draw it forward through the stitch to form a new stitch. To work a purl stitch, with the yarn in front of the work, insert the right needle into the top of the first stitch on the left needle from back to front, pass the yarn from right to left around the point and draw it through the stitch away from you to form a new stitch.

Knit stitch, with right hand carrying the yarn.

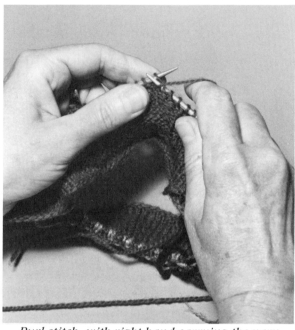
Purl stitch, with right hand carrying the yarn.

English/American System

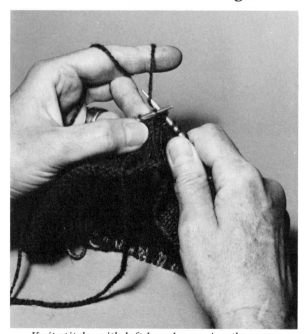
Knit stitch, with left hand carrying the yarn.

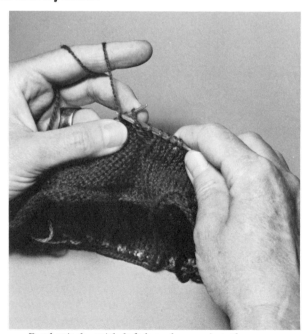
Purl stitch, with left hand carrying the yarn.

Continental/German System

The Continental Method. In Continental knitting, hold the yarn in the left hand and tension it around the other fingers. I tension by wrapping it twice around my forefinger. To work a knit stitch, insert the right needle front to back from below, as in the English method; but since the yarn is directly behind the stitch, pass the point over the yarn and scoop it up and forward through the stitch to form a new stitch. For a purl stitch, the yarn is held in front by moving the left forefinger toward you. The needle is passed from back to front through the loop on the needle, the point swings over the yarn and scoops it downward and back through the stitch to form a new stitch. Both stitches, particularly the purl, require supple wrist action, rather than the finger or arm action of the English method.

Equipment

Knitting needles have improved over the years. Today's circular needles have almost replaced double point needles, and have gone a long way toward replacing the long single pointed needles common since the beginning of the 20th century. For knitting in the round, circular needles eliminate the transition from one needle to the next that so often frustrates the beginner. For sweaters, circular needles can be used for everything except small tubular areas such as the lower sleeves. A 16″ circular needle can be used for the upper sleeve and neck ribbing, and a 24″ one will handle the body of all but the largest sweaters, which might require a 29″ needle.

A welcome modern tool is the magnetic row keeper. This is a metallic board with flexible magnetic strips to mark your place in a pattern. Place your knitting chart on the board and position the strips directly *above* the row in progress so you can see the chart of completed rows and find your place more easily.

Another invaluable tool is the handy pocket calculator. Knitting in the old way means working each sweater from a standard plan instead of from a line-by-line pattern; a calculator simplifies the mathematical calculations necessary (and I'm sure our folk knitter would have used one if she could). As modern knitters, we work with many different yarns in a variety of styles from many cultures; having all the necessary numbers memorized is all but impossible. But knowing some basic formulas and working out the calculations for each sweater will guarantee a good fit.

In addition to the basic equipment mentioned above, you will need a standard cable needle for some of the textured designs, a blunt tapestry needle with a large eye, a few sharp needles, a tape measure, and some markers. Markers can be yarn loops or the little rings sold especially for knitting, but I've found that an assortment of split rings used by fishermen work better. They're inexpensive, available in a wide range of sizes, and thin but durable; they slip easily from needle to needle, and are very smooth so that they won't snag the yarn. Another item often missing from today's knitting bag is a pad of graph paper. Before lengthy printed knitting patterns became common, graph paper was standard equipment for knitters. Five-square-to-the- inch paper is a good choice for charting textured designs, but knitter's graph paper is better for working color stranded designs. It is divided into rectangles instead of squares to give a better representation of the finished pattern, in which a stitch is wider than it is long. Finally, you'll need colored pencils or felt-tipped markers for making your own charts. Correction fluid is also useful, both to correct errors and to change the design on the chart without redoing the entire piece.

Basic Knitting Techniques

Most folk sweaters use only a few of the most basic knitting techniques, so these are the ones I will discuss here. If you need more in-depth knitting instruction, both Mary Thomas' *Knitting Book* and Jacqueline Fee's *The Sweater Workshop* are excellent references.

Casting on. There are many ways to cast on in knitting, but they can be divided into two basic types: the elastic cast-on and the firm cast-on. An elastic cast-on makes an edge with give, as for a standard ribbing. A firm cast-on is appropriate when the edge needs to be smooth and durable but not particularly elastic, as for a divided welt edge or a corrugated ribbing where the knit stitches are in one yarn and the purl stitches in another. There are a number of ways to do both types of casting on, but I'll just give you ones that I've found most useful.

A *twisted loop cast-on* forms a highly elastic, durable edge. It's very difficult to draw the stitch too tightly, so you need not work with doubled needles or a larger size as is the case with many cast-on techniques. To start this two-strand technique, draw an initial strand of yarn from the ball—about 1″ for each stitch in a medium weight yarn. Working in the English method, with the yarn tail in the left hand, the strand coming off the ball in the right hand, and a needle in the right hand, here's what you do:

1. Pass the yarn across the left palm, around the back of the thumb and out through the V formed between the thumb and forefinger. Hold the yarn coming off the ball taut with the right hand, while the last three fingers of the left hand secure the tail.

2. Bend the left forefinger forward, across the yarn.

3. Moving the thumb forward, swing the forefinger downward, scooping the yarn up and around the finger.

4. Extend the forefinger, which now has a loop with an extra twist at its base encircling it.

5. Slip the thumb out, dropping the yarn off the thumb.

6. Knit the loop off the left forefinger onto the needle. Now you're back where you started, ready to pass the yarn around your thumb again.

Repeat these six steps for each stitch required. This cast-on can also be worked in the continental manner; just be sure to have that extra twist at the base of the loop before you knit it off.

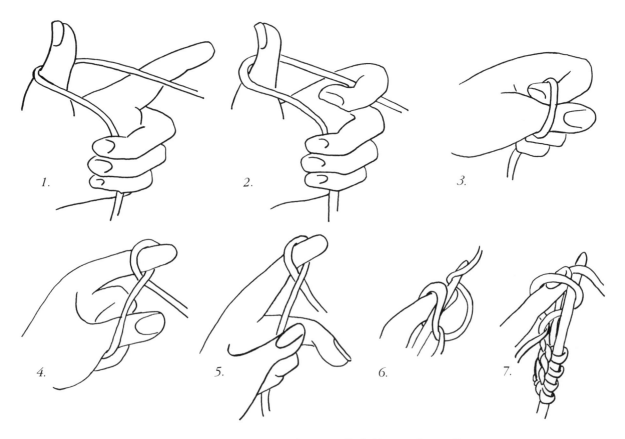

Twisted Loop Cast-On in English/American System

This twisted loop cast on can also be worked Continental, inserting an additional twist into the usual cast on, as follows:

1. Begin with a slip knot for the first loop.

2. With the tail wrapped around the thumb and the strand coming off the ball around the forefinger of the left hand, go *under* the loop around the thumb, bringing the back loop forward.

3. With the tip of the needle, reach out and catch the yarn on the forefinger, drawing the yarn through the twisted loop.

4. Slip the twisted loop off of the thumb, drawing the loop on the needle snugly.

5. Repeat these steps for each cast on loop.

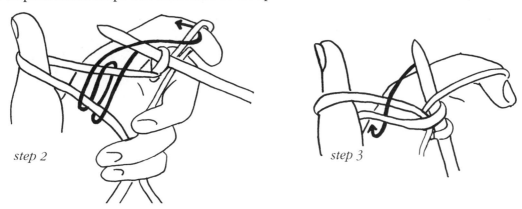

step 2   *step 3*

Twisted Loop Cast-On in Continental System

A *cable cast-on* forms a very firm, non-elastic edge. It is made with two needles and a single strand of yarn. Make a slip knot near the end of the yarn and place it on the left needle. Then:

1. Knit a stitch, but instead of dropping the old stitch from the left needle, leave it there and transfer the new stitch to the left needle also.

2. Pass the right needle *between* the two loops on the left needle and knit a stitch, again slipping the new stitch off the right needle onto the left. Repeat this step for each cast-on stitch required.

Cabled Cast-On

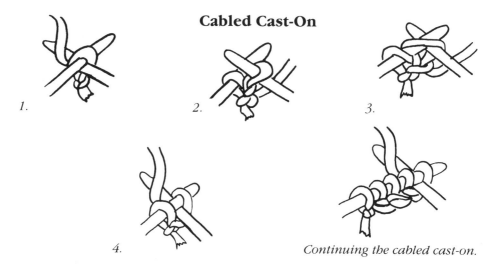

1. *2.* *3.*

4. *Continuing the cabled cast-on.*

Backward loop cast-on.

A third method of casting on, which is used when the work is already in progress, is the simplest of all. This technique involves placing a series of backward loops on the needle as shown in the figure at left.

As folk sweaters are usually worked in the round, you will be casting on to either circular or double pointed needles. In either case, you must be very careful not to twist the cast-on edge when you join the two ends. Check carefully to be sure that the cast-on edge lies neatly within the circle of the needles, as shown in the illustration. If you allow this cast-on row to twist, you'll end up with a figure-eight tube, not a circular one! If you've used a cable cast-on, reverse your needles before joining the circle, as the yarn will be coming off the left needle when the cast-on is complete. Or, knit the first row, joining the circle at the end of this row rather than at the cast-on edge.

Stitches cast on circular needle; cast-on edge lies neatly within circle.

Cast-on with double point needles; care must be taken to avoid twisting the stitches between the needles.

Increases

Structural increases should be invisible rather than decorative. I like the raised increase. As the name implies, the new stitch is raised from the row directly beneath the working row. With the tip of the left needle, slip down *between* the stitches of the preceding row, lifting the interconnecting yarn, twist it to form a loop, and knit this loop as shown. This increase is only slightly directional, but even so, it is best to work the increases in pairs, one leaning left and one leaning right, in a symmetrical piece.

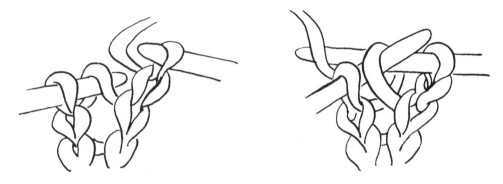

Make one raised leaning left.

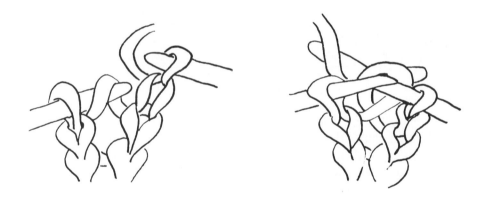

Make one raised leaning right.

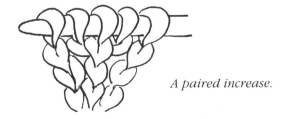

A paired increase.

Decreases

There are three basic decreases: left, right, and balanced.

The simplest, knit two together (K2tog or [◢]) leans to the right and is worked just as its name implies, by knitting two stitches as one.

Knit two together (K2tog) decrease. This decrease leans to the right.

For the sake of symmetry, a decrease which leans to the left is necessary to balance a K2tog. Slip one stitch knitwise, slip another stitch knitwise, and then pass the left needle tip back through the reversed loops, knitting the two off together. This decrease is called slip, slip, knit (SSK or [◣]). Or you can achieve similar but less balanced results by simply knitting two stitches together through the back.

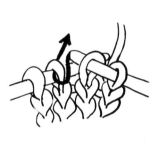

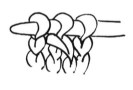

Slip, slip, knit (SSK) decrease with each stitch slipped knitwise, then knit off as one. This decrease leans to the left.

A double, or balanced, two-stitch decrease is made by slipping two together knitwise, knitting the next stitch, and slipping the two slipped stitches together over the knit stitch (S2 knitwise, K1, P2SSO or [▲]).

Balanced Double Decrease

Slip 2 together knitwise.   *Slipped stitches on right needle.*   *Knit next stitch.*

Pass 2 slipped stitches over together.   *Balanced double decrease.*

Binding Off

The philosophy of the folk knitter is to avoid any unnecessary binding off, as this is the first area on any knit garment to show wear because of the inflexibility of usual bound off stitches. The standard binding off technique is to knit the first two stitches, slip the first stitch over the second stitch, knit the third stitch, slip the second stitch over, etc., until all the stitches are removed. (If working in ribbing or a pattern stitch, maintain the pattern instead of knitting each stitch.) The binding off should always be worked loosely so it will be flexible. To insure some degree of flexibility, you can work this edge with a larger needle.

Binding Off Two Sets of Stitches Together

Put right needle through both stitches.

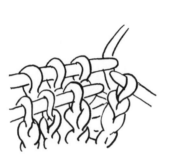

Knit 2 stitches off together.

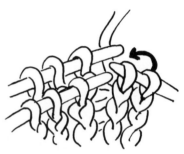

With 2 knit stitches on right needle, slip first stitch over second stitch. Continue in this manner until all stitches are removed.

For a slightly more elastic bind-off, knit two together, slip the new stitch back onto the left needle, K2tog, slip the stitch to the left needle, and so on until all stitches have been bound off.

Binding off two sets of stitches together is a useful technique to eliminate a sewn seam, for instance at the shoulders. Do this on the wrong side for a smooth finish, or bind off on the right side to create a decorative ridge.

Grafting

Grafting, sometimes called "Kitchener stitch", is a technique for joining the stitches of two edges together invisibly. Butt the two pieces together, right sides up, and make the join with a strand of yarn about four times as long as the join threaded on a tapestry needle. The joining yarn follows the same path as a row of knitting. With an equal number of stitches on each needle, follow this sequence, beginning with the first stitch on the front needle:

1. Bring the tapestry needle through the front stitch purlwise, leaving it on the knitting needle.

2. Bring the tapestry needle through the back stitch as if to knit.

3. Bring the tapestry needle through the front stitch as if to knit, and slip this stitch off the needle. Bring the tapestry needle through the next front stitch as if to purl, again leaving it on the needle.

4. Slip the back stitch off the needle purlwise, and then bring the tapestry needle through the next back stitch as if to knit, leaving it on the needle.

Repeat steps 3 and 4 until all stitches have been worked. Remember that the tapestry needle must enter each stitch twice. You may need to adjust the tension on the loops of this grafted row so that it matches the rest of the knitting.

Grafting two sets of stitches: following the path of the stitches, the needle passes through each stitch twice.

Selvedge Edges

Many knitters prefer to slip the first stitch of each row, because this firms up the edge and minimizes its tendency to curl. This is particularly desirable when working an edge that will be picked up later and worked in ribbing, such as along a cardigan front. It also gives a neat chain stitch edge that can be seamed flat. It's optional at other edges; in fact, if you're going to be picking up in stockinette stitch, you'll have to move one row in from this chained edge to have the correct number of stitches to pick up from, and this makes extra bulk.

Picking Up Stitches

Early folk knitters avoided seams, often picking up stitches on an edge instead. The process of picking up stitches is simply that of knitting through the fabric edge. With the right side of the work facing you and starting from the right edge, pass the needle through the first stitch. Knit the 'stitch' as usual, and proceed across to the left.

Stitches are wider than they are high, so you will pick up fewer stitches than the number of rows. The number of stitches you need for a given length can be calculated, or an average can be worked. The actual number is calculated from the gauge: for example, at 5 stitches and 7 rows per inch, a length of 10″ would require 50 stitches to be picked up, evenly spaced on the 70 rows, or 1 stitch for every 1.4 rows. If you don't want to bother with figuring the actual number, an average for stockinette stitch, regardless of gauge, is to pick up stitches from four rows, skip one row, and repeat. Working four out of five rows results in your stitches being grouped in fours, which makes counting easy.

Since ribbing is elastic, I recommend picking up for ribbing by picking up stitches at the end of two rows, skipping a row, and repeating. Working two out of three rows is a handy grouping for either K1,P1 or K2,P2 ribbing.

If a selvedge edge has been worked by slipping the first stitch of each row, the number of stitches at the edge is half the number of rows. If you're picking the edge up in ribbing, working one stitch in each of the selvedge stitches is satisfactory. If the edge is being picked up for stockinette stitch, the simplest pick-up is to ignore the slip stitch selvedge and pick up the second stitch from the edge.

Yarn Splicing

Splicing is a technique for joining a new ball of yarn without a knot. Untwist both plies at the end of the old ball and the beginning of the new one. Break them off into different lengths, overlap the old and new yarns about 3″, and twist the ends together slightly, following the twist of the yarn. This technique is especially good for handspun or softly spun yarn, as it makes an invisible join and eliminates the irksome project of working in loose ends. The technique can also be used for mill-spun yarns, although if your yarns are very smooth and regular, the splicing might show. In this case, end off the old ball at the side seam and pick up a new ball there, leaving the tails to be worked in later. To work in yarn ends, use a sharp pointed needle, piercing through the back of the stitches rather than tucking the yarn ends under them, so that the ends won't work loose. Dividing the plies and working each in separately keeps the ends from adding bulk. To splice a bulky single ply yarn, taper about 4″-6″ of the ends by pulling out fibers. Overlap and twist the two together.

Buttonholes

Buttonholes to accommodate any size button can be made with a two-row technique. First, bind off the number of stitches necessary on one row. When you come to the bound off stitches on the next row, turn the work and cast on replacement stitches using the cable cast on, adding one additional stitch. Instead of slipping the additional cast-on stitch onto the left needle, turn your work again and continue the row, knitting the last cast-on stitch and the first garment stitch together. Use the K2tog or SSK, depending on the direction of slant necessary.

Short Rows

Knitting short rows shapes a knitted garment invisibly. Short rows can be used to make the neck higher in back than in front and to shape the shoulders. The technique is covered in detail with the Full Yoke Sweater plan which beings on page 56, and with the Shaped Sweater on page 64.

Perpendicular Joining

This is a very valuable technique that can be used to eliminate a bound-off edge and sewn seam. You can use it in any situation where there is a perpendicular junction, such as on some neck edges and on saddle shoulders. It is covered in detail with the Saddle Shoulder Sweater plan on page 49.

Diagrams and Charts

Until the mid 1800s, knitting patterns were put on charts, kept on samplers, or passed on verbally. Knitted patterns have a rhythmic repetition, with each row related to the previous one. For this reason, patterns are more easily learned and followed when they're presented visually. On a graph paper chart, each square represents a stitch. Almost any pattern, including intricate textured designs, can be put on a chart. All you need is a set of symbols. most of the following symbols are widely used and understood; they are derived from a variety of sources.

Knitting Symbols

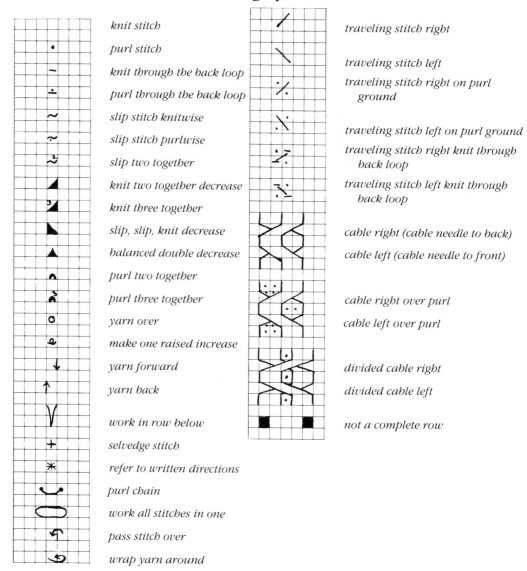

	knit stitch
•	purl stitch
−	knit through the back loop
⊥	purl through the back loop
~	slip stitch knitwise
~	slip stitch purlwise
	slip two together
	knit two together decrease
	knit three together
	slip, slip, knit decrease
▲	balanced double decrease
∩	purl two together
	purl three together
o	yarn over
	make one raised increase
↓	yarn forward
↑	yarn back
V	work in row below
+	selvedge stitch
*	refer to written directions
‿	purl chain
⬭	work all stitches in one
	pass stitch over
	wrap yarn around

/	traveling stitch right
\	traveling stitch left
	traveling stitch right on purl ground
	traveling stitch left on purl ground
	traveling stitch right knit through back loop
	traveling stitch left knit through back loop
	cable right (cable needle to back)
	cable left (cable needle to front)
	cable right over purl
	cable left over purl
	divided cable right
	divided cable left
■ ■	not a complete row

In addition to pattern charts, schematic diagrams are helpful tools. Refer to the chart here for a set of symbols for various structural elements and construction details that can be used to develop plans for any sweater size and style. Knitting in the old days meant passing sweater plans down from one generation to the next. But in a mixed culture such as ours, the entire heritage of ethnic sweaters from around the world can be at our fingertips with the use of these simple visual records.

Diagramming Symbols

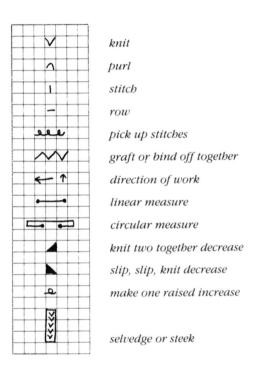

knit

purl

stitch

row

pick up stitches

graft or bind off together

direction of work

linear measure

circular measure

knit two together decrease

slip, slip, knit decrease

make one raised increase

selvedge or steek

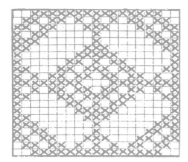

Sweater Plans

When you've taken the time to knit a sweater by hand, and especially if you've spun your own yarn, you want a garment that is unique and distinctive, yet in a style that you can wear year in and year out. Traditional designs and patterns that have been handed down from generation to generation generally fit these criteria. The simple, classic shapes of folk sweaters also are the basis for many handknit fashion sweater variations today. Thus understanding and using traditional sweater styles opens the door to both ethnic and high fashion knitting.

The following sweater plans are based on gauge and on the percentage system first devised by Elizabeth Zimmermann. Understanding and using them will help you become an independent designer, freed forever from that mass-produced look.

Gauge

Gauge is the number of stitches and rows in a given measure. It is usually expressed as stitches and rows per inch, but it's best measured over at least 4″ (10 cm). The vital figure is the number of stitches. The number of rows per inch is less important since the length can easily be adjusted by measuring your work as you go—although it's helpful to know the number of rows when calculating depths on your sweater diagrams so you can plan the best position for design elements. The number of stitches per inch is important because it's a measurement of width; you are committed to a certain number of stitches when you cast on, and the width can't be changed as easily during the knitting of the garment.

To determine gauge, first knit a sample. Always knit the sample in the pattern that you'll use in the garment, whether textured or color stranded. A good swatch size for ultrafine to fine yarns is 5″ × 5″; for medium to heavy yarns make it 7″ × 7″, and for bulky to chunky yarns 9″ × 9″. After knitting the sample, either bind off or remove from the needle and lightly block it. Lay a ruler over the surface, and place a pin at each end of the area to be measured. Count the number of stitches between the pins and divide by the number of inches between the pins. Repeat this in several places on the swatch, and take the average of all the measurements. This is *your* gauge for *this* yarn on *these* needles.

As most of the knitting in an ethnic sweater is worked in the round, it's a good idea to knit your the sample for measuring gauge in the round, too.

Many knitters' tensions vary when knitting round or flat.

Your sample swatch should have the hand and visual appeal you want. If it doesn't, try again. For a firmer, denser fabric, use smaller needles; for a softer, more elastic fabric, use larger ones. Remember that firm yarns work up best into firm fabrics, while softer yarns are more suitable for soft fabrics. You wouldn't, for instance, want to knit a fluffy angora yarn into a tight, stiff fabric. Tentative gauges for various yarn weights and needle sizes are given in the "100 Yarn Rule" on page 11.

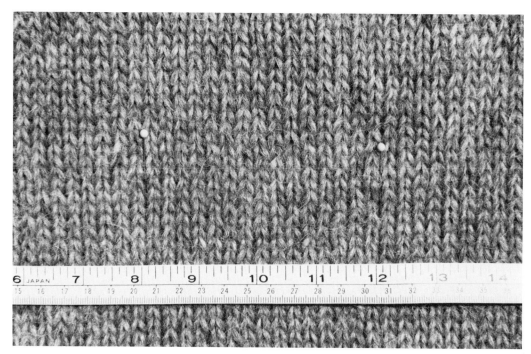

Measuring gauge over 4" by counting stitches between two pins. Accuracy is important, as gauge affects all your calculations in knitting.

An accurate determination of your gauge is *the* single most important measurement in knitting, as all subsequent work is based on this figure. Therefore, this measurement must be accurate even to the half-stitch.

The Percentage System

The percentage system is a simplified method of pattern drafting. It is based on one part of the garment being proportional to another part, just as one part of the body is proportional to another. The use of percentages makes the calculations easier, especially if you use a pocket calculator. The percentage system not only determines proportions for your sweater, but it allows you to convert inches to number of stitches or rows, and vice versa.

Using the percentage system, all the calculations for a basic sweater are based on one measurement: the chest measurement plus ease. This becomes the circumference of the sweater, and can be stated:

$$\text{Circumference} = \text{Chest} + \text{Ease} = 100\%$$

The amount of ease can vary according to preference: 2" for a snugly fitting sweater, 4" for a "comfortable" one, or 6" for a loosely fitting sweater.

Sweaters today usually have a snug ribbing at the hips, so this area requires fewer stitches than the circumference of the sweater. You'll need about 90% of the circumference for the hip band of a snug or comfortably fitting sweater, or 80% if the sweater is very loose fitting or if you want a very snug hip band.

Your head is smaller than your chest, and so the neck opening is proportionally smaller than the sweater circumference. For an adult crew neck sweater, the head opening is typically 40%-45% of the circumference (use 45% if you've allowed only 2″ ease). Use 50%-55% for the neck opening of a child's sweater. These percentages will vary with different necklines.

A typical upper sleeve is 50% of the circumference of the sweater. This percentage will also vary depending on the style of the sleeve. Since the wrist is proportional to the upper arm which is proportional to the chest, the wristband measurement can also be correlated to the circumference; 20% is usually about right.

All of the above measurements are of circumference. Other necessary dimensions have to do with length and can be determined with a tape measure. Here's an example of how to figure the numbers you need for an adult with an actual chest measurement of 36″, plus 4″ of ease, knit at a gauge of 5 stitches per inch and 7 rows per inch.

Chest + ease = Circumference × sts/inch = 100% of stitches
36″ + 4″ × 5 sts/in = 200 stitches
Circumference = 40″ = 200 sts = 100% of stitches

All other width measurements are then a function of circumference. Using the hip band as an example:

Hip Band = 90% of C
HB = .90 × 40″ = 36″
HB = .90 × 200 stitches = 180 stitches

Sample Sweater Plan

An example of a simple sweater showing the use of both the percentage system and the diagram in designing should help you understand the system.

Gauge = 5 sts and 7 rows per inch
Circumference = 100% = 40″ = 200 stitches
Hip Band = 90% = 36″ = 180 stitches
Neck = 40% = 16″ = 80 stitches
Upper Sleeve = 50% = 20″ = 100 stitches
Wristband = 20% = 8″ = 40 stitches

Above the hip band, you must increase from 90% to 100%, in this example a 20 stitch increase from 180 stitches to 200 stitches. This requires an increase after every ninth stitch (180 / 20 = 9). Going from a 90% to a 100% circumference *always* involves an increase after every ninth stitch, no matter what the total number of stitches is. For a snugger hip band, you would increase from 80% to 100%, from 160 to 200 stitches for the above example, an increase of 40 stitches, or one increase after every fourth stitch (160 / 40 = 4).

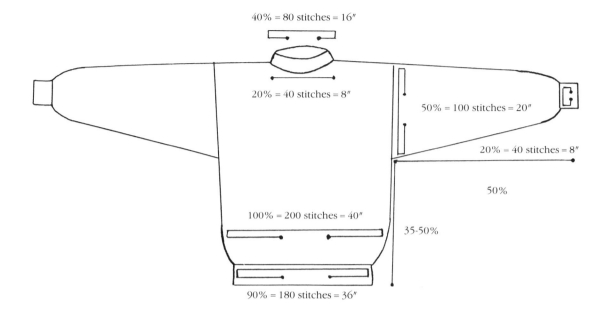

40% = 80 stitches = 16"

20% = 40 stitches = 8"

50% = 100 stitches = 20"

20% = 40 stitches = 8"

50%

100% = 200 stitches = 40"

35-50%

90% = 180 stitches = 36"

The neck in the example is 40% of the circumference, 80 stitches, half for the front neck and half for the back. Therefore, the center 40 stitches on both front and back must be set aside for the neck opening.

The sleeves, if knit from the wrist to the underarm, require an increase of 60 stitches. The increases, one on each side of a center underarm "seam" line stitch, will need 30 rows. How often these increase rows occur depends on the length of the sleeve. Assuming you want the increases to occur smoothly along the whole length of the sleeve, you can determine how often to increase by converting the length of the sleeve from wrist to underarm into the equivalent number of rows. For example, if the sleeve length is to be 20" total, minus 2" for the wristband, an increase of 60 stitches must be made over a distance of 18" 126 rows (18" × 7 rows per inch = 126 rows). An increase must be made every .6" or every 4.2 rows (126 rows/30 increase rows = 4.2 rows). The practical way to accomplish this is with an increase after every fourth row, or every ½". An increase on every fourth row will usually result in a 30% increase from the wrist to the underarm for the 50% sleeve.

Other sleeve variations can be increased with an average row figure: the 50% sleeve on every fourth row, the 40% sleeve on every fifth row, and the 35% sleeve on every sixth row. If the sleeve is worked from sleeve cap to wrist, reversing the direction of the work, start at the underarm and increase at these same intervals.

If you choose to work the *average* number of rows between increases, rather than the *actual* number, the sleeve will not work out exactly. You'll have to make some adjustments, but since the knit fabric is very accommodating, they won't affect the final appearance of the garment. These minor adjustments are fairly simple. If, when working from the wrist up, the sleeve shaping occurs too rapidly, stop increasing when you've reached the correct number of stitches. The finished sleeve will have a longer area of full width:

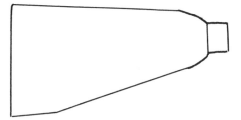

If the increasing occurs too slowly, begin to increase on every other row in the last section. The upper sleeve will have a shorter area of full width.

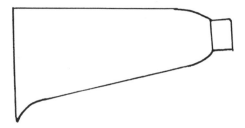

When working from upper sleeve to wrist, if the decreases occur too rapidly, stop decreasing when you've reached the correct number. The sleeve will have a longer area fitting somewhat snugly.

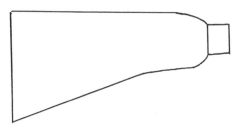

If the decreasing occurs too slowly, take out all the extra stitches in the last row before the wristband. The sleeve will be slightly bloused.

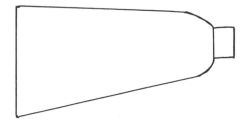

Through diagramming, you can illustrate construction details with the use of symbols. The diagram below indicates an increase after every ninth row above the hipband (from 90% to 100%), with the neck opening stitches set aside and the shoulder seams grafted or bound off together. It also shows the sleeve worked from wrist to upper sleeve, with an increase on every fourth row (from 20% to 50%) and bound off into the armhole. This is a simple example, but it illustrates the use of construction symbols.

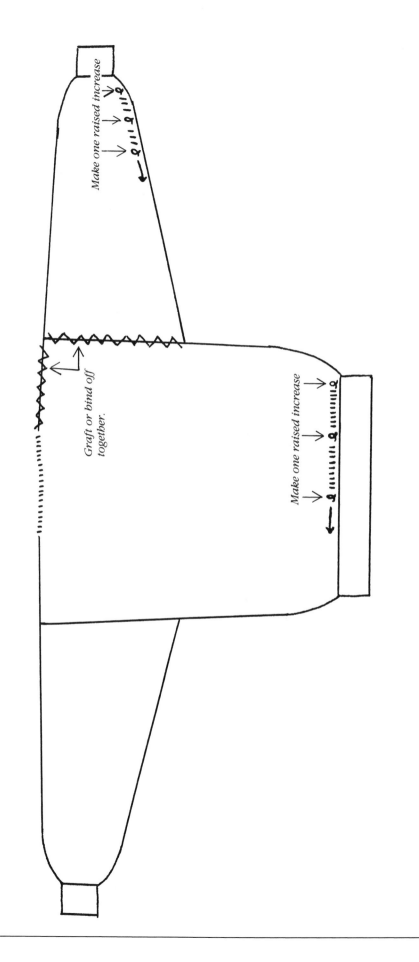

Make one raised increase

Graft or bind off
together.

Make one raised increase

A Sweater Diagram Showing Construction Techniques

For efficiency and easier knitting, incorporate all figures, symbols, and dimensions into a single diagram. Plan the entire sweater, showing all measurements in both inches and stitches or rows. Make the diagram as complete as possible, positioning design motifs to best advantage. Planning ahead doesn't mean that adaptations and adjustments won't be necessary or possible. As your work progresses, you'll see the need for little changes, and you'll be able to handle them.

Sweater Shapes

At this point, we've covered the percentage system and diagramming in very general terms without getting into the wide variety of sweater styles possible. Each sweater shape, as it has evolved through the years, requires its own plan. The next section gives plans for bodies, sleeve shapings, and neck openings, beginning with the earliest shapes and carrying through to modern garments. Some plans are only minor variations on previous ones, but in sequence they show how shapes and techniques seem to have evolved. All the diagrams are drawn to the same scale, so you can trace different features and combine them into one garment. Special techniques peculiar to each style are illustrated.

The sweater plans in this section have been adapted for modern fit. They aren't necessarily reproductions of the old ethnic sweaters, but they are firmly founded on traditional shapes and construction techniques. To adhere to every detail of a style of a hundred years ago would be of little practical use today, except for historical interest.

The percentages used in each of the plans are based on an 'average' fit. They can be adjusted for personal preference. Keeping records of your experiments will allow you to find the percentages you need to get a perfect fit in every sweater.

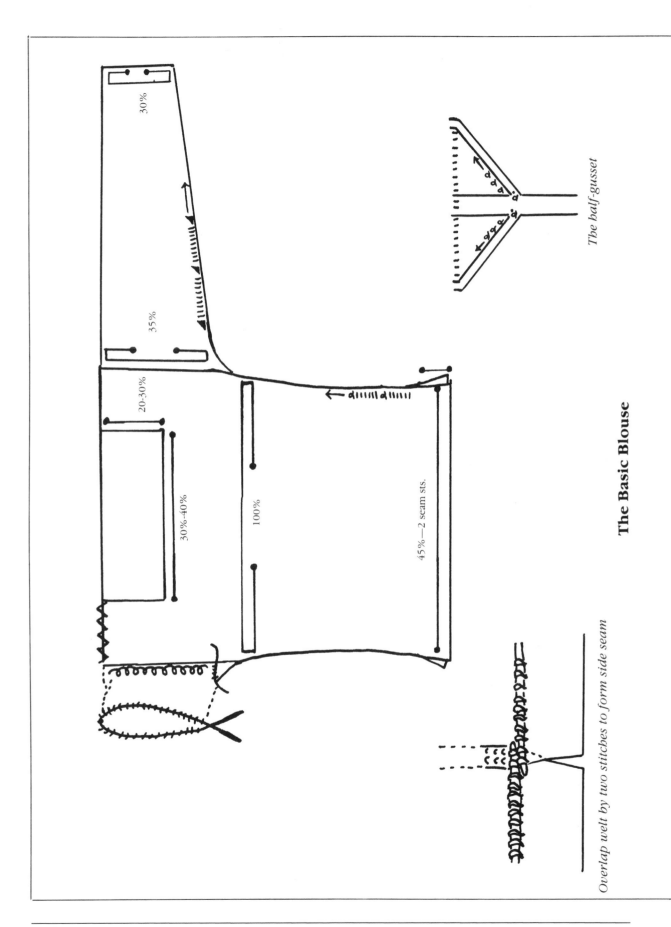

30%

35%

20-30%

30%-40%

100%

45% — 2 seam sts.

The half-gusset

Overlap welt by two stitches to form side seam

The Basic Blouse

1. The Basic Blouse

The earliest sweater shapes were based on rectangular woven garments: boxy, with gussets providing underarm shaping and a split welt for the hem treatment. Possibly the earliest of these garments was the Danish *natrøje*, a night shirt or undergarment which evolved into the brocade blouse of Danish folkwear. It was very snugly fitted, taking advantage of the greater elasticity of knitting compared to weaving.

To make a basic blouse, begin knitting two welt hem sections. When they are the desired depth, join them to form a circular tube by overlapping two stitches. The overlapping stitches reinforce the join and set up a seam marker for the front and back sections. To overlap the stitches, lay the front section over the back and work the last two stitches of the one piece and the first two stitches of the other together. The two stitches should be purled to make a visible but fake seam. This seam marker is continued up to the underarm where it will allow the neat insertion of a half-gusset.

As you knit the body of the garment, increase at each side of the purl seam stitches at regular intervals. How often the increases occur depends on the additional ease necessary for the bust compared to the waist and the length from waist to underarm.

When you've reached the proper depth, insert a half-gusset. To do this, begin with a purl increase on each side of the two purl seam stitches. These new purl stitches will become seam stitches between the armhole and the sleeve. The gusset must increase in size rapidly, so make a K1 increase immediately after and just before the P1 seam stitches on every round while continuing the P2 seam stitches. Continue increasing until the depth of the half-gusset is about half its width. At this point, place the half-gusset stitches on a strand of yarn. Then divide the front and back bodices and work them separately, maintaining the P1 seam at the edge of each armhole.

After you've worked enough depth for the armhole, graft or bind off the shoulder stitches together. Pick up the sleeve stitches around the armhole, including the half-gusset stitches, and work down to the wrist, decreasing to taper the sleeve. The half-gusset is now part of the sleeve, with the purl seam stitches maintained and decreases paired on each side to reduce the width of the sleeve. As the lower sleeve is not snugly fitted, paired decreases on each side of the seam occur at greater intervals than is typical on modern sweaters. Finish the sleeve hem with a welt to match or coordinate with the bodice hem.

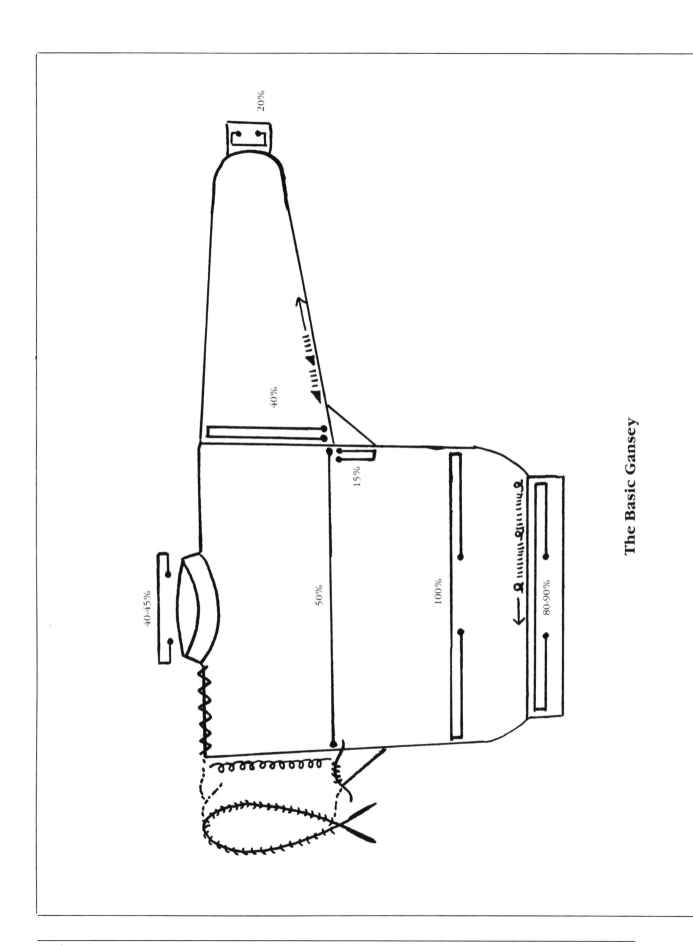

The Basic Gansey

2. The Basic Gansey

The gansey is a modification of the "Basic Blouse". Early ganseys were fairly long garments with a split welt hem treatment, but this has since been replaced with a ribbing band by most knitters.

The work begins at the hip band. Knit a ribbing band about 2″ wide (a K2,P2 ribbing holds its shape better than a K1,P1 ribbing), increasing to the 100% circumference after completing the band. A two-stitch purl marker is worked at each side seam. If you used a K2,P2 ribbing, continue a P2 rib from the band up each side for the seam stitches.

Work even on the body stitches until you reach the underarm. Start the gussets by working a raised increase between the two purl stitches. This style gusset is a longer diamond-shaped piece. Work it by making paired increases on every *other* row to the desired depth. Put the gusset stitches on a strand of yarn, and work the front and back separately, still maintaining the purl seam stitch up the armhole. Bind the shoulders off together. Often this was done on the right side for a decorative raised finish.

Pick up the sleeve stitches along the edge of the armhole, including the gusset stitches. Work the sleeve down to the wristband, decreasing the gusset on every other row until all its stitches are used up. Maintain the purl seam right into the wristband, which is worked in the same ribbing as the hip band.

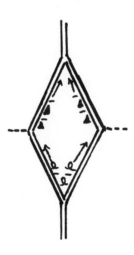

The underarm gusset

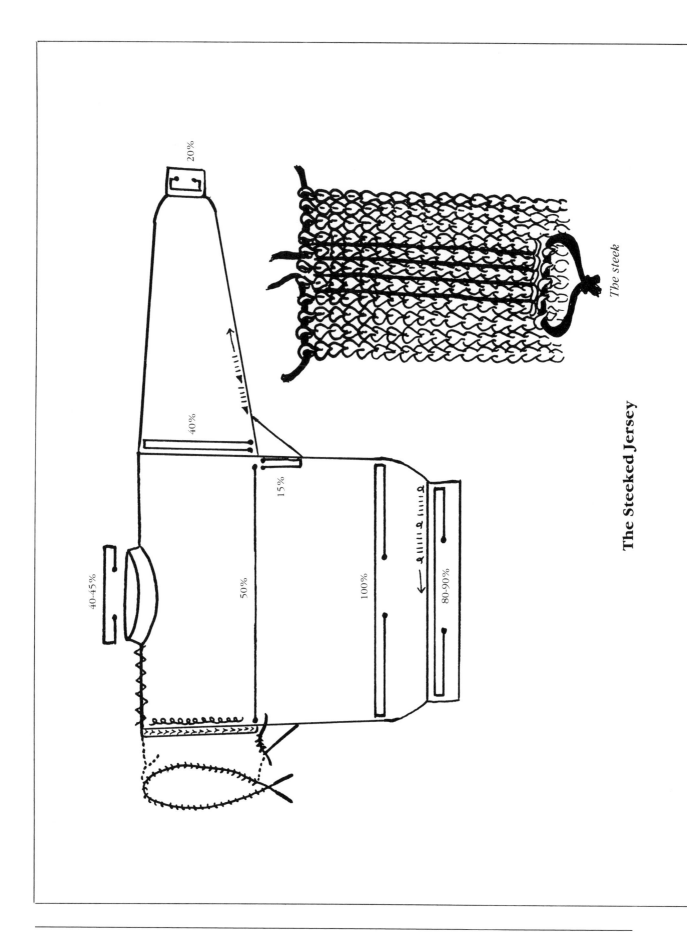

20%

40%

15%

40-45%

50%

100%

80-90%

The steek

The Steeked Jersey

3. The Steeked Jersey

The earliest folk sweaters were knit in one color, using textured designs for visual enrichment. At some point knitters began to use color stranding techniques which double the fabric thickness, creating a warmer garment with designs in contrasting colors. These sweaters were knit in the round. Various treatments of the armhole allowed the tube to be slashed for the insertion of the sleeve.

On Fair Isle, early color stranded sweaters followed the gansey shape with gusset. For a color stranded sweater, start at the hip band and work up to the gusset, omitting the purl side seams. The gusset can be worked in the main color or with two colors worked alternately for a speckled effect. Changing colors every other stitch gives an interesting pattern while eliminating long strands of yarn carried at the back of the gusset. When you reach the centermost point of the gusset, transfer the gusset stitches to a holder. The back and front are joined with a Scot's steek and the work is continued in the round up to the shoulder.

'To steek' translates 'to close', and that is just what the Scot's steek was designed to do, close the gap. It closes the tube for continued circular knitting above the gusset. After removing the gusset stitches to the yarn holder, bridge the gap that's left by casting on with the backward loop cast-on. Five stitches is about right for medium to heavy yarns and seven stitches for fine to medium yarns. The steek technique is not recommended for heavier yarns which would be too bulky to seam. Cast on in alternate colors. Continue to work in the round, alternating the colors of the steek stitches in each row and from one row to the next. After you've worked the armhole to its full depth, cut the steek. (Yes, *cut* the steek!) In early days, when the time came to insert the sleeve, this area was simply slashed down the middle stitch. Today we usually use a double row of machine stitching on each side of the center stitch before slashing. After you've completed the sleeve, you'll see that the steek folds neatly back against the body of the sweater where it can be secured with a closely spaced herringbone stitch. To make the herringbone neater, use only one ply of yarn and work small stitches with a sharp needle, catching only the back of the sweater stitches.

After cutting the steek, bind off together or graft the shoulder stitches, including the steek stitches. Pick up the sleeve stitches along the armhole, including the gusset, and work down to the wristband. Since the body of the sweater is worked from the hip band *up* and the sleeve is worked from the shoulder *down*, reverse the color stranded designs in the sleeves. To align the body and sleeve patterns when the sweater is on, begin the sleeve with the same part of the pattern that appears at the midpoint of the armhole or slightly below. This type of sweater has a dropped shoulder line, and to work the part of the body pattern on the sleeve often results in an unpleasant jog in the design when it's worn.

The Shaped Steek

4. The Shaped Steek

As greater emphasis began to be given to garment shaping, the dropped shoulder in the color stranded gansey shapes gave way to a moderately fitted shoulder shape. On Shetland Island sweaters the steek was still used, but the gusset was omitted.

Working even from the hip band to the underarm, remove a number of underarm stitches (about 5% of the circumference at each side) and place them on strands of yarn. Close the gap with a steek as described above, working in alternating colors, and continue to work in the round, decreasing every or every other row on each side of the steek until enough stitches have been removed to bring the armhole in line with the edge of the shoulder. After slashing the steek and joining the shoulders, pick up the sleeve stitches at the armhole and work from the shoulders down to the wristband, *or* work the sleeve from the wristband up to the shoulder and sew the sleeve in stitch by stitch. The former technique was more common.

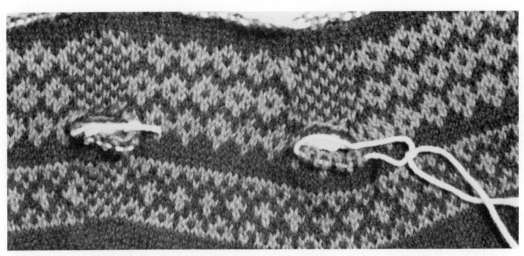

A straight steek is on the left, and a shaped steek on the right.

Steeks after cutting; note how the shaped steek opens at an angle because of the decreases that have been made.

The Locked Turning Stitch

5. Sweater With Locked Turning Stitch

At some point, many knitters working in color stranded patterns began to feel that slashing techniques were inferior, and began to work back and forth across the yoke area. Working back and forth in color stranding is slower in all but the bulky yarns, as the natural rhythm of the repetition of design is broken when you have to turn the work. On the other hand, it eliminates finishing cut edges and consequent seam bulk. Bulky weight yarns are best worked back and forth, because a slashing technique would result in unpleasantly bulky seams. Also, since there are fewer stitches in the heavier weight yarns, working them back and forth is not so tedious. To make the edges neat when working back and forth, you should use a locked turning stitch.

In bulky sweaters, a true gusset was seldom used. Rather, a half-gusset with a short series of paired increases was incorporated at the underarm to provide ease. Begin the increases about 3″ below the armhole and repeat them about every third round. These underarm ease stitches will be removed to a holder when you've reached the underarm depth.

With locked turning stitches at the armhole, the front and back will be worked flat. Divide the work into front and back, designating the last stitch of each as a locked stitch. When you come to the end of the row, knit all the colors of that row together into this stitch. Then turn and work the first stitch of the following row in the main color. Locking all the colors into the final stitch of each row insures that the stitches in the next row will be smooth and even. There will be no gaps or holes in the work, since all the yarns will go from one side to the other.

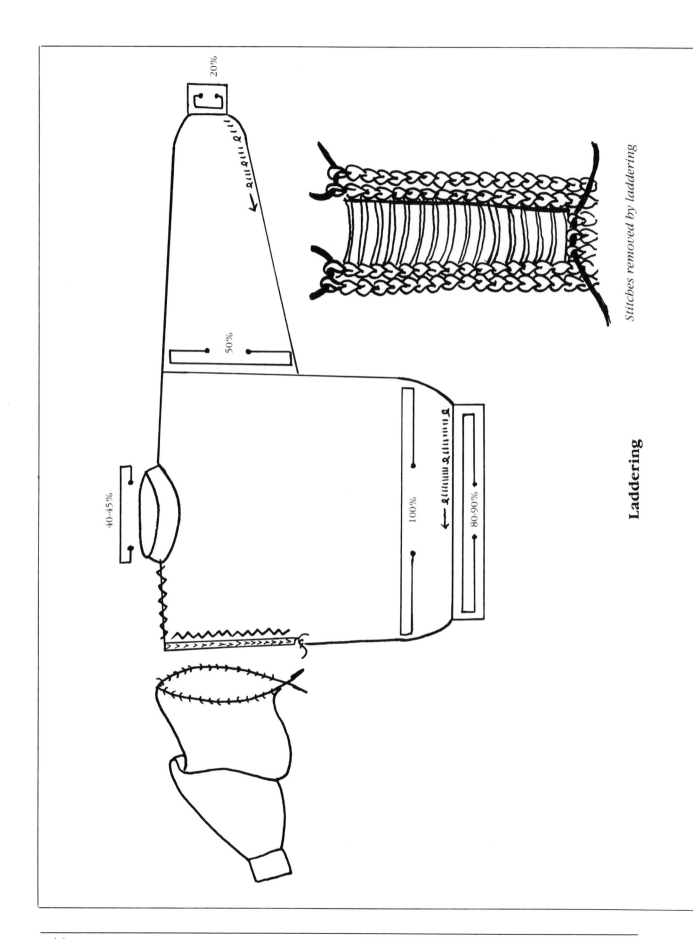

20%

50%

40-45%

100%

80-90%

Stitches removed by laddering

Laddering

6. Sweater With Laddered Openings

In Northern Europe, the slashing technique often involved laddering the stitches (raveling down several rows of stitches), cutting them, and tying them off in pairs. Today's knitter can machine-stitch along the edge of the laddered stitches before cutting, using a zipper foot to get close to the stitches. For a neat appearance, the ends should all be tucked in.

You must knit *every* color in *every* stitch designated for laddering. To ladder the stitches, designate about three 'platform' stitches at the base of the armhole. Run a yarn through the platform stitches, but *do not remove* them from the needle. Continue to work in the round, maintaining pattern, knitting all yarns of each row in every stitch of the ladder. When you've reached the full depth of the armhole, remove the designated stitches from the needle and ladder them down to the platform stitches.

Today, stitching around the armhole with a double row of machine stitching is more common than laddering. After stitching, the armhole is slashed. This doesn't work as well as laddering because it doesn't provide a set of platform stitches; without them, the underarm stitches at the turn are awkward, bulky and less durable. If you feel that the old laddering technique is too time consuming, use the Scot's steek instead. Though it's not traditional in the Scandinavian countries, it's a better alternative than the modern stitch and slash method.

Whichever way you choose to create your arm openings, begin at the hip band, work the sweater to the underarm, close the armhole either with a steek across three to five platform stitches or a ladder above three to five platform stitches. Work the sleeves from the wristband to the shoulder. They can be bound off into the armholes while incorporating the platform stitches, or you can sew them in stitch by stitch with the platform stitches grafted. This latter method is somewhat less bulky and more flexible. In either case, place all the stitches of each sleeve on a string and divide them evenly into the armhole. Then bind off or stitch, whichever you please.

The shoulder seams can be grafted. In some old sweaters, a small gusset was inserted in the shoulder seam just next to the neck opening.

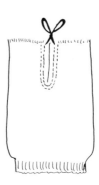

stitching and slashing the modern Nordic way

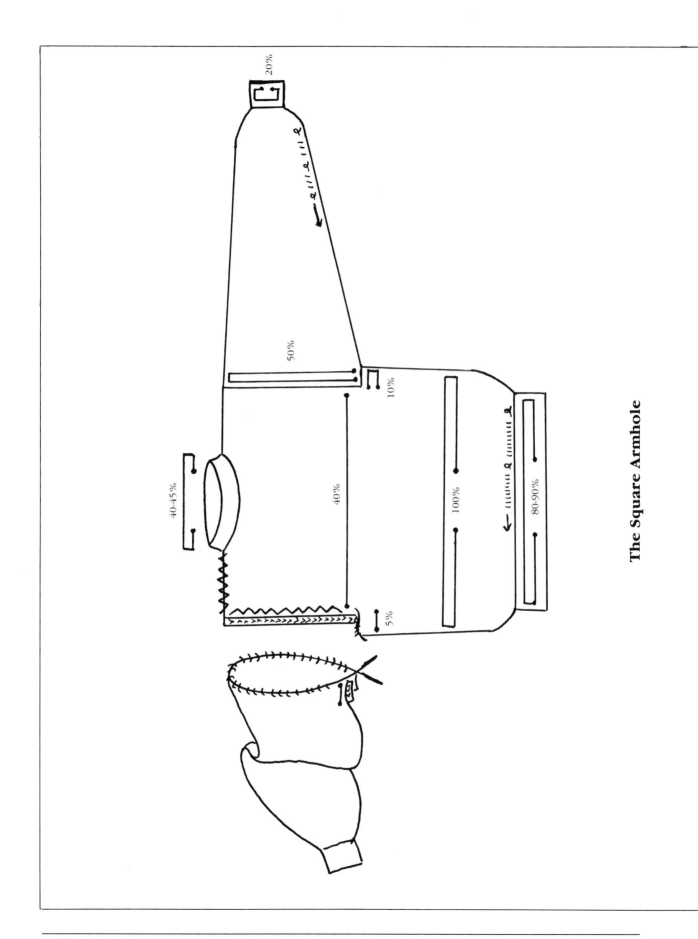

The Square Armhole

7. The Square Armhole

When the shaping of shoulders became more common, the Northern European laddering technique was modified, with enough stitches in the platform to create a square armhole going straight to the point of the shoulder. The upper sleeve is modified to fit into the opening. It is slashed at the underarm to a depth equal to half the total platform width. When opened out flat, the slashed area on the sleeve equals the total underarm width. The sleeve can be bound off into the armhole or stitched into place.

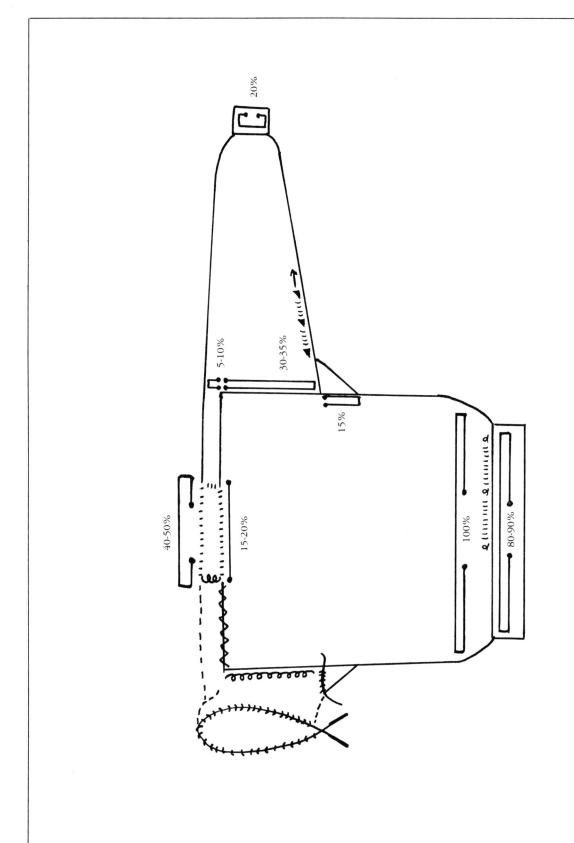

The Saddle Shoulder With Gusset

20%

5-10%

30-35%

15%

40-50%

15-20%

100%

80-90%

48

8. The Saddle Shoulder With Gusset

A style common to parts of Great Britain is the saddle shoulder, also called a shoulder strap. This style was often used in Scottish ganseys. The body of the sweater is knit as for the Basic Gansey. Begin at the hip band and knit to the gusset. Divide the work evenly front and back, working each to the base of the neck where the stitches are divided into three parts: the centermost for the neck, and two side sections for the shoulders.

Place the front shoulder stitches of one shoulder on a needle, and the back shoulder stitches on another. At the neck edge, cast on the number of stitches required for the shoulder strap onto the right hand needle. Knit the first stitch on the left needle, and pass the last cast-on stitch over this stitch. Turn and purl back across to the last shoulder strap stitch, purling it and the first shoulder stitch off together (P2tog). Turn and knit back to the last shoulder strap stitch, knitting these two stitches together with the slip, slip knit decrease (SSK). The front shoulder and back shoulder are being joined by casting on a strip between the two pieces, which is worked at right angles to the front and back. One shoulder stitch at the *end* of each shoulder strap row (not at both ends of each row) are worked with the strap stitches. In a textured design, work the design stitches across all but the first and last stitches. The first stitch is worked as a SSK and the last as a P2tog. While this might sound confusing, it will become clear as you do it.

To make the shoulder strap cast-on invisible at the neck edge, cast on and work one row in a contrasting yarn, preferably a slick cotton, before continuing with the sweater yarn. When you are ready to knit the neck band, remove the contrasting yarn, pick up the resulting loops, and knit the neck band.

When all of the shoulder stitches have been worked into the edge of the shoulder strap, pick up the stitches around the armhole and gusset and continue working the sleeve down to the wristband.

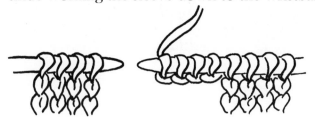

Cast on stitches at neck edge

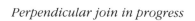

Perpendicular join in progress

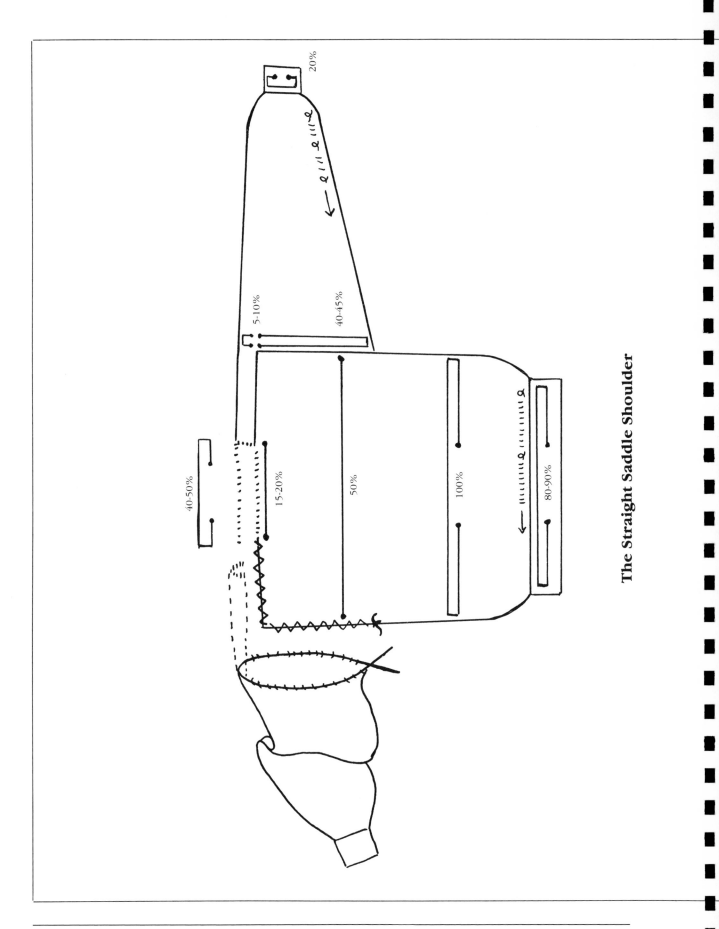

The Straight Saddle Shoulder

9. The Straight Saddle Shoulder

The straight saddle shoulder was used in the earliest Aran fishing shirts. Modern patterns give the instructions in flat knitting, but many knitting authorities think that these garments were knit in the round, since circular knitting was long established in that part of the world. As working in the round is the easier technique, this is the procedure I will describe.

Begin at the hip band and work to the armhole. Divide the work evenly, front and back, with three to five platform stitches at the underarms to make the turning a bit smoother and more durable. Work the front and back flat to the neck, and then divide each into three sections for the neck and two shoulders.

Knit the sleeves from the wrist up. When you reach the shoulder, work across the stitches designated for the shoulder strap, and set them aside on a yarn holder. Starting at one shoulder edge, with the right sides of the sleeve and armhole together, bind off the sleeve stitches, working through the ends of the row at the armhole. Work around the sleeve and back to the shoulder strap stitches. To complete the shoulder strap, put the shoulder strap stitches and one set of shoulder stitches on one needle, and the other set of shoulder stitches on the other needle. Work back and forth, doing a perpendicular join—a P2tog or a SSK—at the end of each row as described above. Continue until no shoulder stitches are left.

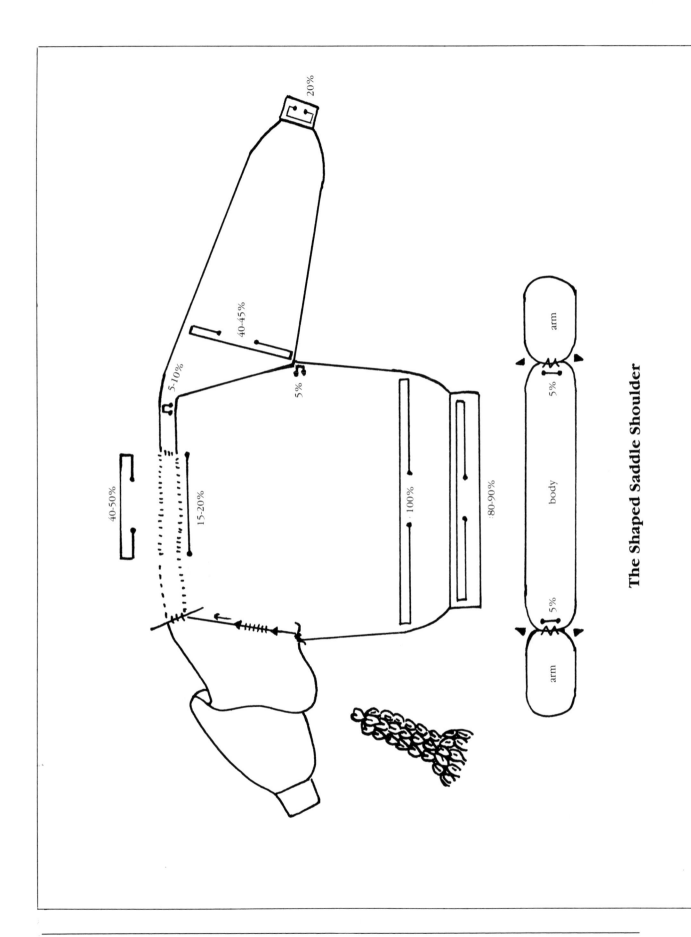

20%

40-45%

5-10%

5%

40-50%

15-20%

100%

80-90%

arm

body

5%

5%

arm

The Shaped Saddle Shoulder

10. The Shaped Saddle Shoulder

The saddle shoulder can be modified to shape the shoulder and reduce some of the boxiness of the style. Work the sweater from the hip band to the underarm as before, and remove the underarm stitches to a holder for grafting later. Set the sweater body aside and work the two sleeves from the wrists to the underarms. On each sleeve underarm, set off an equal number of stitches onto yarn holders for grafting to the body. Now join all three pieces on one large circular needle. Knitting the last body stitch and the first sleeve stitch together reinforces this joining; place a marker before this stitch, marking it as a seam stitch. Work about six or eight rows even. Begin to decrease at each seam marker on every sixth to eighth round (the wider spacing between decreases results in a more pronounced shoulder strap). A balanced double decrease is the best choice for this seam: slip 2 tog knitwise, K1, P2, SSO. The stitch just before the seam stitch and the seam stitch are slipped together knitwise, the next stitch knitted, and the two slipped stitches passed over the knit stitch together.

When you've reached the desired armhole depth, place the remaining sleeve stitches on a straight needle, leaving the rest of the stitches on the circular needle. Work a perpendicular join, working the saddle while joining one loop from the body on each side. Refer to "Saddle Shoulder With Gusset" for details on this technique. Continue to work in this way until you've reached the neck; then repeat the process with the other shoulder.

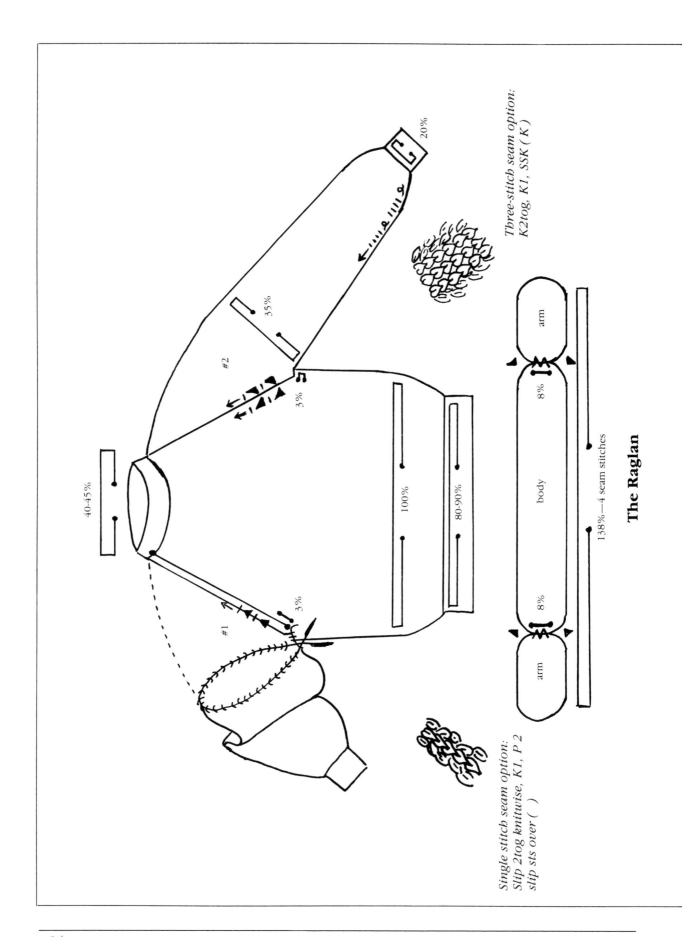

20%

35%

#2

3%

40-45%

100%

80-90%

3%

#1

Three-stitch seam option:
K2tog, K1, SSK (K)

arm

8%

138%—4 seam stitches

body

The Raglan

8%

arm

Single stitch seam option:
Slip 2tog knitwise, K1, P 2
slip sts over ( )

11. The Raglan

The raglan shape, of fairly recent origin, rapidly replaced the saddle shoulder sweater; this is particularly evident in modern Arans. This sweater is worked to the underarm just as the shaped saddle shoulder, removing the underarm stitches to be grafted, and joining the body and both sleeves on a circular needle as before. Work about 1"-1½" as established, and then begin to decrease at each seam with a paired decrease on every other round. My preference is to K2tog, knit the seam stitch, then SSK; this creates a decorative three-stitch seam. An alternate method is the balanced double decrease in which the stitch just before the seam stitch and the seam stitch are slipped together knitwise, the next stitch is knitted, and the two slipped stitches passed over the knit stitch together. This results in a neat one-stitch seam. Continue decreasing until the sleeve stitches are all used up, shaping the neck as you go.

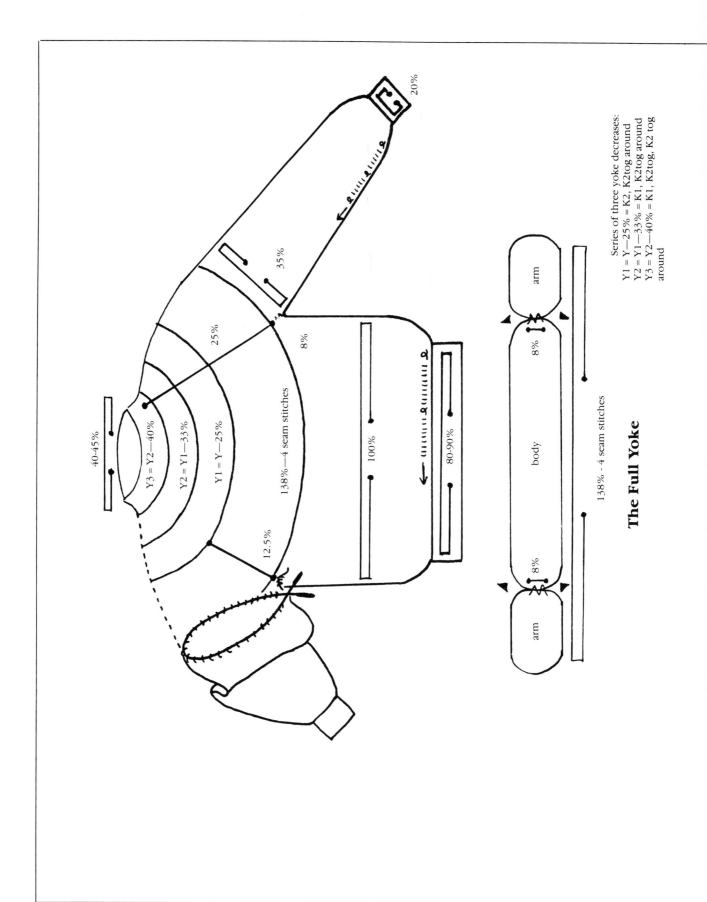

20%

35%

25%

8%

Y3 = Y2—40%

Y2 = Y1—33%

Y1 = Y—25%

40-45%

138%—4 seam stitches

12.5%

100%

80-90%

The Full Yoke

arm

body

arm

8%

8%

138% - 4 seam stitches

Series of three yoke decreases:
Y1 = Y—25% = K2, K2tog around
Y2 = Y1—33% = K1, K2tog around
Y3 = Y2—40% = K1, K2tog, K2 tog
   around

12. The Full Yoke

The circular yoke sweater, among the youngest of the traditional shapes, is thought to have been developed by the Bohus knitting cooperative in Sweden in about 1940. Although it looks complicated, it is easy to work. As with the raglan, the body and sleeves are worked separately to the underarm where they are joined on a large circular needle, knitting the first and last stitch of the sleeve and body together and placing a marker at each join. The yoke section can be worked in several ways; one way for heavier yarns and/or full yoke designs, and others with more shaping for finer yarns and/or shallow yoke designs.

To work the full yoke and/or heavy to bulky weight sweater of the type popularized in the mid-1950s in Iceland, establish three rounds of decreases within the design. The depth of the yoke, from underarm to neck front, is equal to about 25% of the body circumference. Divide this depth into three sections. The first decrease round occurs halfway to the neck. On this round you will remove 25% of the stitches by working K2, K2tog all the way around. When you've worked two-thirds to three-fourths of the yoke depth, eliminate 33% of the remaining stitches with a K1, K2tog round. Just before you reach the base of the neck, work the final decrease round, reducing the stitches by 40% with a K1, K2tog, K2tog round.

Decreasing this way in concentric circles works for any design that can be divided into three bands. Or you can work five decrease rounds in the yoke, following this sequence:
1. Decrease by 10% (K10, K2tog)
2. Decrease by 15% (K5, K2tog)
3. Decrease by 20% (K3, K2tog)
4. Decrease by 25% (K1, K2tog)
5. Decrease by 33% (K1, K2tog, K2tog)

Regardless of how you do the decreases, the neck opening should be 40%-45% of the circumference.

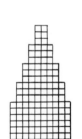

If you're working a continuous pattern, you'll have to adapt the decreases to fit the pattern, though the general location and rate of decrease remains the same. To work the decreases into the design, first determine the number of rows you'll need to work the entire depth. Next, think of the yoke as a cone, and divide it into 16 or 20 equal parts around the base. (Choose a number that works well with your total number of stitches.) For any sweater, there will be a given number of stitches at the base of this cone, and a given number that you're aiming for at the top or neck; the difference between these two numbers is the number of decreases you need to make.

On graph paper, mark out the number of stitches at the base of each cone segment, count the number of rows in the yoke, and mark off the number of stitches at the center top of the cone segment. (Any leftover stitches can be removed at the base of the neck ribbing.) Remember that the decreases should occur in the upper half of the yoke. Look at this example of how a cone segment might look, and then experiment with placing decreases in the cone segment of your pattern.

cone division of yoke

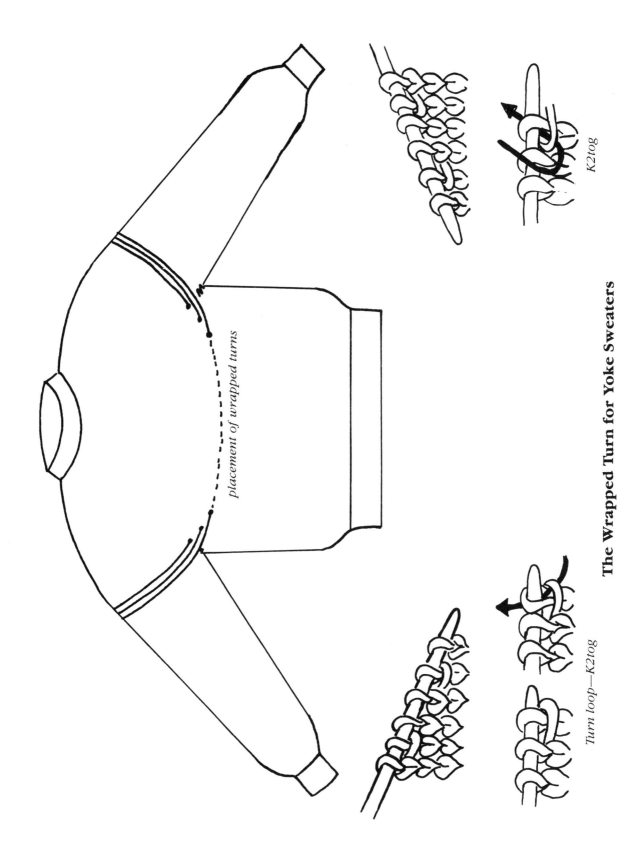

placement of wrapped turns

K2tog

Turn loop—K2tog

The Wrapped Turn for Yoke Sweaters

The result of following this procedure is a round yoke, with front and back neck equal in depth. For better fit, you can shape the neck so it's higher in back by using short rows, working more rows around the arms and back of the sweater than in the center front. A few rows below the beginning of the yoke pattern, knit across the front, the sleeve, the back, and the second sleeve. This returns you to the sweater front, but don't knit across it yet. Using a wrapped turn, reverse the work and knit back across the sleeve, back, and other sleeve where you reverse again. Work these short rows three to five times for heavier yarns. Work all the wrapped turns evenly spaced about five stitches apart on the garment front, immediately below the design.

To work the wrapped turn on the knit side:
- work up to the turning stitch,
- slip the turning stitch to the right needle,
- reverse the work,
- take the yarn to the back,
- slip the turning stitch back again onto the right needle,
- bring the yarn to the front, and
- purl across.

To work the wrapped turn on the purl side:
- slip the turning stitch from the left needle to the right
- reverse the work,
- bring the yarn to the front,
- slip the turning stitch back onto the right needle,
- take the yarn to the back, and
- knit across.

In each case, the slipped turning stitch has been encircled with the working yarn.

After you've worked as many short rows as necessary to bring the back of the garment to the right height relative to the front, start the yoke design, beginning at a back sleeve seam stitch. When you reach the wrapped turns slanting off to the left, knit the wrap and the turning stitch *together*. When you reach the wrapped turns slanting off to the right, slip the turning stitch knitwise to the right needle, place this stitch on the left needle (the loop is now reversed) and knit off the wrap and the reversed loop of the turning stitch *together*. Work the sweater yoke design, following the decreasing sequence that you've chosen.

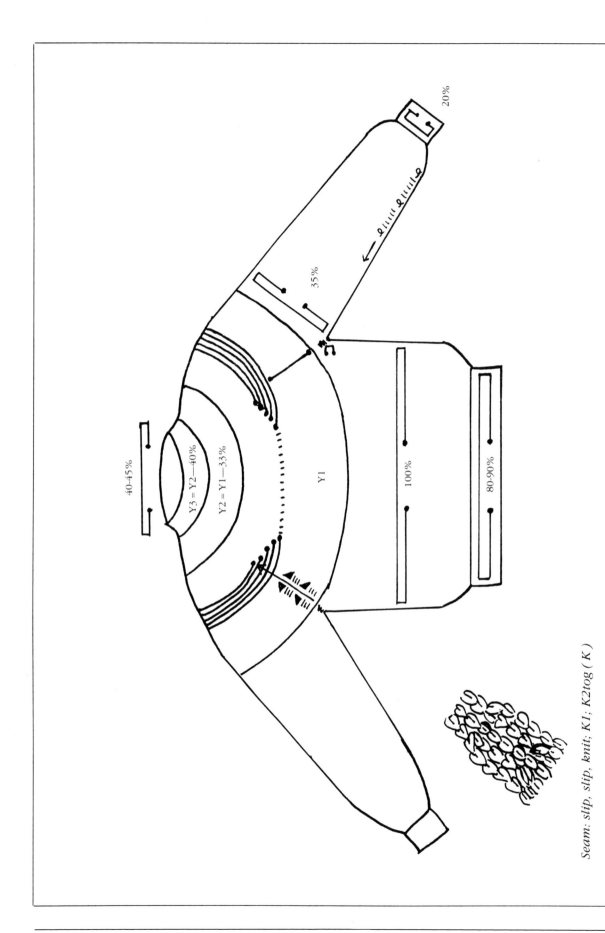

20%

35%

40-45%

Y3 = Y2—40%

Y2 = Y1—35%

Y1

100%

80-90%

The Shoulder Yoke

Seam: slip, slip, knit; K1; K2tog (K)

13. The Shoulder Yoke

A shoulder yoke sweater is shaped the same as a full yoke sweater, but the patterning doesn't start until halfway up the yoke. There are two ways to work this style.

In the first way, proceed as for the full yoke sweater, joining the sleeves and body into one unit with a K2tog join. Continue to work even on these stitches until you've completed half of the yoke depth; then incorporate all the decreases in concentric circles or into the design as described for the full yoke, using at least five short rows at the base of the design if the yarn is fine.

The other way is to remove some of the underarm fullness for a smoother fit—often desirable in finer yarns. After joining the sleeves and body with K2tog stitches, which are designated as seam stitches, knit three rounds even. Decrease one stitch on each side of the seam stitch. To make this as inconspicuous as possible, work the decreases this way: SSK, knit the seam stitch, K2tog. Repeat this paired decrease at each seam stitch on every fourth round until you've completed slightly less than half of the yoke depth. At this point, start working short rows as described in the "Yoke Sweater" (with fine yarns, you'll need more short rows to bring the back up to the desired height), and at the same time continue decreasing at the seams. When you've finished the short rows, discontinue decreasing at the seams; at this point you've reduced the stitches by approximately 25%, so only two additional decrease rounds are necessary.

Start working the yoke design at a *back seam stitch*, working the wrapped turns off as for the "Yoke Sweater", working even, until you've completed two-thirds to three-quarters of the total depth. On the next round, decrease the stitches by 33% with a K1, K2tog round. Continue to work even to the base of the neck, where you reduce the stitches by 40% with a K1, K2tog, K2tog round. The neck is now 40%-45% of the total circumference.

The decrease rounds can be worked any number of ways; don't be afraid to experiment. Just remember that the goal is the orderly decrease of stitches in the upper half of the yoke, with the rate increasing as you get closer to the neck. Regardless of how you work the decreases, the resulting neck opening should be 40%-45% of the original 100% circumference.

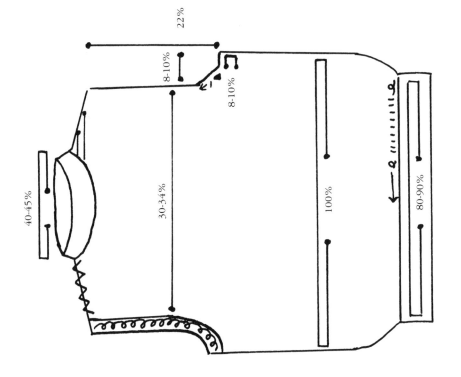

Shaped Vest

14. The Shaped Vest

Early in the 20th century, shaping knitwear more closely to the body became important; shoulder seams were slanted, and sleeve caps shaped to fit. Flat knitting began to replace circular knitting. Many knitters don't realize, though, that having shaped shoulders and sleeve caps doesn't necessitate working each piece separately and them seaming them together. After all, seams are both less durable and more unsightly than the smoothly shaped continuous surface that you can achieve knitting in the round. The body and sleeves of most any sweater can be worked in the round up to the underarm. The work can then be divided into front and back and worked back and forth; or if a color stranded design is involved, the openings can be steeked, with the garment shaped on each side of the steek. One simply adapts the old way to accommodate the new shape.

Little adaptation of the old way is necessary for a sleeveless vest. The depth of the armhole and the underarm width are slightly increased to accommodate a ribbing or some other type of finish for the armhole.

Working from the hip band to the underarm, bind off the underarm stitches. Working on the front and back separately, decrease at both ends of every other row for the curve at the base of the armhole, and then work straight to the shoulder. Slope the shoulder in increments of three to five steps, depending on the weight of the yarn (the heavier the yarn, the fewer the steps). To slope the shoulder, divide the total number of shoulder stitches by the number of steps you need, and work using the short row technique as follows.

Assuming there are a total of 30 stitches in the shoulder, and that you're working the shoulder front, work from the neck edge out to the last ten stitches of the armhole, execute a wrapped turn, and return to the neck edge. Turn and work to the last 20 stitches at the armhole edge, wrap and turn and return to the neck edge. The shoulder shaping is now complete, but you'll have to work an additional row across the entire shoulder to bring the wrapping stitch into line with the other stitches. Place these shoulder stitches on a holder while you work the corresponding shoulder back. Then with both sets of stitches—shoulder front and back—right sides together, bind off together or graft to join the two sections.

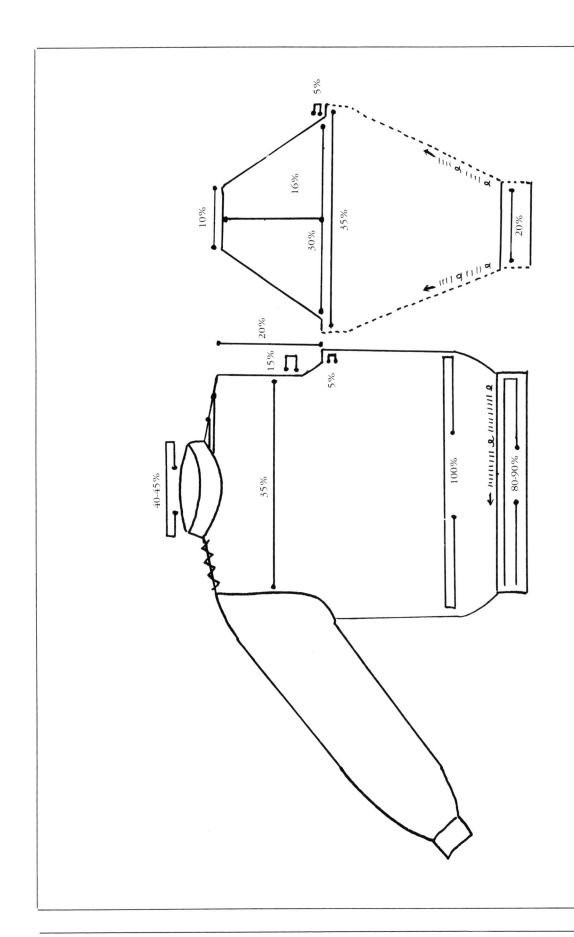

15. The Shaped Sweater

Adding sleeves to the shaped vest requires some variation on the basic vest plan: the depth and width of the armhole needs to be reduced, as the sleeve cap provides a part of the girth necessary for the upper arm. The procedure, except for this adjustment, is the same as for making the shaped vest.

Knit the sleeves in the round, from the wrist to underarm, and then bind off the underarm stitches. Work the sleeve cap back and forth, decreasing at each end of the row as often as necessary to reach the 10% width of the upper cap as shown on the diagram. This decrease usually occurs every other row, with adjustments made in the rows just before the top of the cap. Bind off the cap, and the only finishing you'll find necessary is to fit the sleeve into the armhole and sew it into place with a back stitch. If there is any excess fullness in the sleeve cap, ease it around the armhole for a smooth fit.

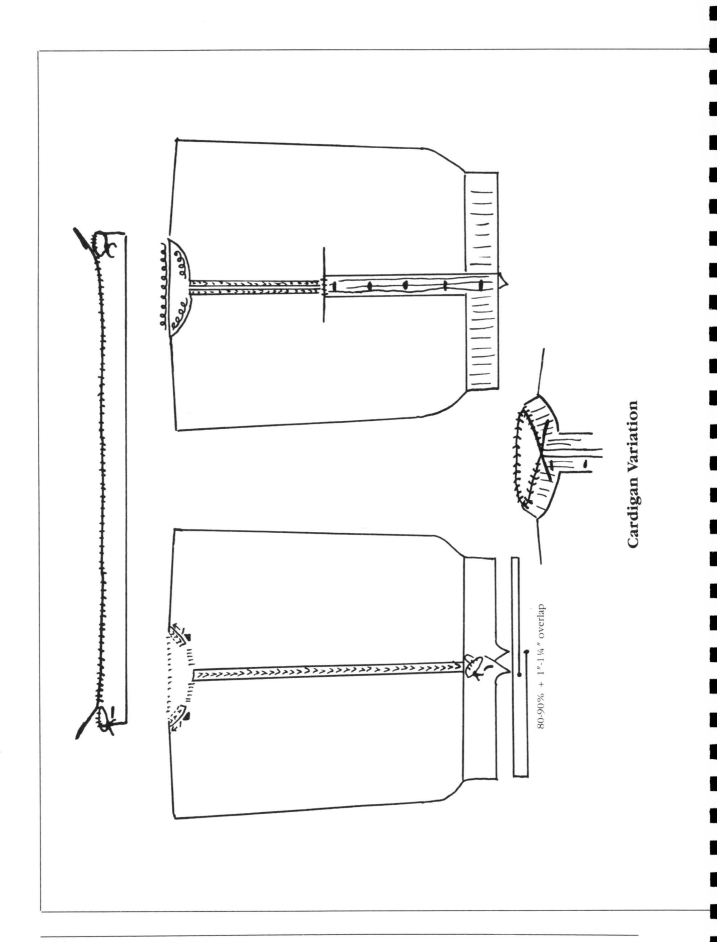

80-90% + 1"-1¼" overlap

Cardigan Variation

16. Cardigan Variations

Cardigans, or knitted jackets, are sweaters with an opening down the front.

Color stranded cardigans can be knit in the round with a steek for the center front, or they can be knit flat with a locked turning stitch. The hip band is knit flat either with or without a front band overlap, depending on the design of the front band. If the front band is to be in ribbing continuous with the rest of the hip band, include enough stitches for it and work buttonholes in the appropriate location. Then put the front band stitches on holders for later and close the front with a steek.

When the sweater is completed and the steek cut, complete the front bands by knitting each up to the neck and hand sewing them to the body of the cardigan. This strip should be slightly shorter than the garment itself; stretch it slightly as you sew it into place. You can also knit the front band onto the body with a perpendicular join, knitting through the edge of two out of three rows and joining with a SSK or P2tog.

To determine the proper location of the buttonholes, work the button side first, stretch it into place and stitch it; then measure to divide the space for the buttonholes. Work the opposite side with buttonholes to correspond. After both sides of the front band are in place, pick up the stitches around the neck opening and finish the neck band.

Another way to make the front band is to knit the hip band flat without providing any extra stitches for the overlap. Steek the cardigan above the hip band, and knit the sweater in the round. After slashing the steek, pick up stitches on a circular needle on one side, around the neck and down the other side. Working back and forth, position the buttonholes when half the depth of the front band is completed. To maintain the corner where the front band meets the neck band, work an increase on each side of a center stitch on every other row.

If the cardigan is worked in a textured pattern, knit the body and front bands in one piece, or with either type of front band described above for color stranded sweaters. The earliest textured cardigans were knit in the round and slashed, and dedicated circular knitters are again returning to using the stitch-and-slash technique. This is a reasonable choice, as the patterns are easier to follow if the right side is always facing you. If you decide to work flat, though, firm up the front edges with a slip-stitch selvedge.

Textured "jackets" of other nations are often waist length and snugly fitted. They have a series of increases on either side of the underarm seam line to accommodate the increase between waist and bust.

In addition to the knit front bands described above, early edge treatments often involved binding the cut edge of a steek with fabric. A crocheted edge also makes an effective finish after machine stitching the steek. Many knitters today knit a tubular cord edge which is easy to work and very attractive. First cast on three stitches on double point needles. Working with the *wrong* side facing you, pick up a stitch through the garment edge and pass the third cast-on stitch over this stitch. *Do not turn* the work, but rather slide the stitches to the other end of the needle and begin the

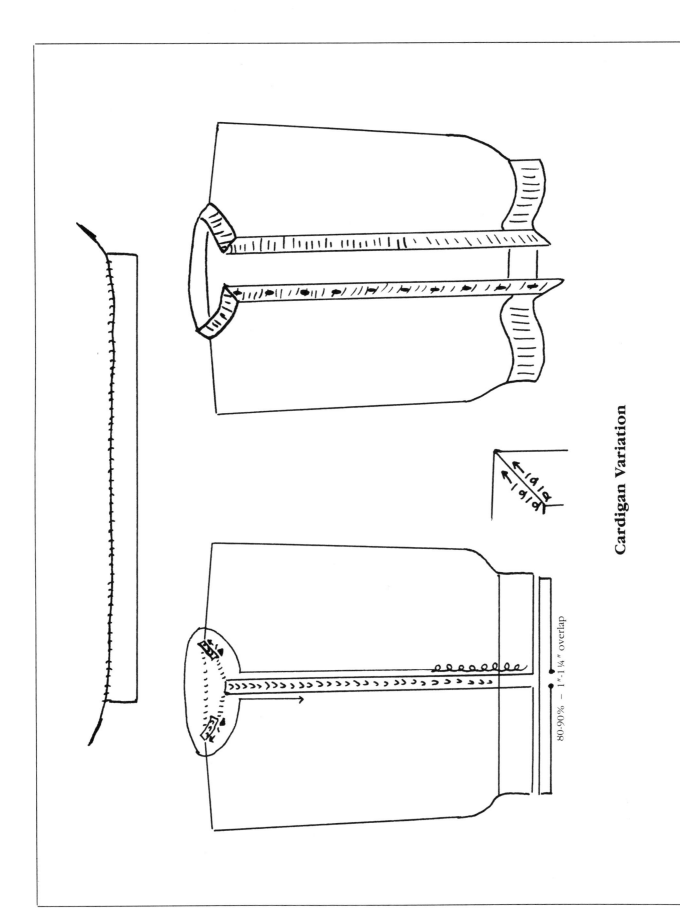

Cardigan Variation

80-90% – 1"-1¼" overlap

next row by knitting the first cast-on stitch. From here on each row is:

K2, sl 1, pick up one stitch through the garment edge, pass the sl st over. All the rows are worked *without turning*, so that a knit tube forms around the edge. If three stitches doesn't cover the edge well, try using four, being careful to pull the yarn snugly between the last and first stitches of the tube. To incorporate buttonholes, work several rows (enough to accommodate your button) without attaching it to the garment. Alternatively, work a second tubular cord edging attached to the first one, leaving a series of un-attached rows between them for the buttonholes. To turn a corner with your edging, work one row unattached on each side of an attached row at the point of the corner. Although it's not a traditional technique, the tubular cord is attractive and functional, and looks at home on many folk designs.

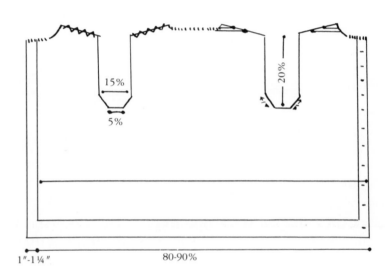

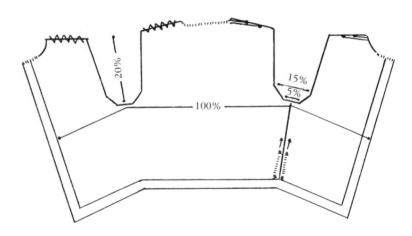

Cardigan Variation

17. Necklines

So far, no mention has been made of neck treatments, though they must be shaped at the same time as the rest of the upper part of the garment. These necklines can be used with any of the preceding sweater types. After you've decided on the sweater to knit, choose a neckline and superimpose it onto the sweater, working it simultaneously with the upper body. You can divide your work when you do the neckline shaping, or you can steek it to maintain circular work.

The crew on a straight neck. Among the earliest neck openings was the crew neck banding set on a straight neck opening, or on a rectangular one with some form of shoulder strap to allow for depth. The neck opening is rectangular; the corners become rounded when ribbing is added. Traditionally, the ribbing band was often knit back and forth with an underlap for buttons to allow it to fit over the head more easily.

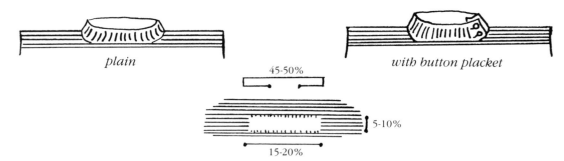

plain   *with button placket*

45-50%

5-10%

15-20%

Crew neck on a shaped neck opening. Today, a crew neck on a shaped opening is usually preferred, as it allows the front of the neck to be lower and thus more comfortable. Pick up stitches around the shaped neck, work to the desired depth, and bind off. Or work double the desired depth, fold the band in half to the inside, and work the neck stitches off one by one with the stitches at the base of the neckline. This eliminates bound-off stitches, and makes a more durable neck treatment when worked loosely. You can extend the length of a crew neck band even more and fold it into a turtle neck; the depth will depend on how high you want the neck to extend.

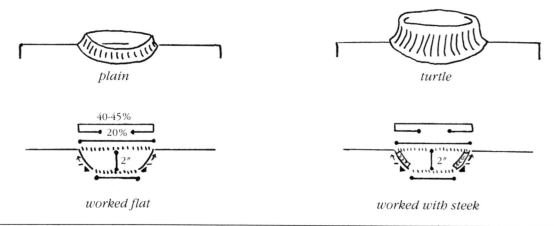

plain   *turtle*

40-45%

20%

2"

2"

worked flat   *worked with steek*

Flat crew neck. A flat crew is a modification of the standard shaped crew; it is wider and therefore accommodates a shirt collar nicely.

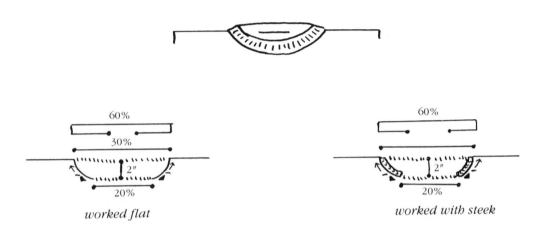

worked flat   worked with steek

The V neck. Working from the bottom up, when you come to the place where the point of the V should be, place the center stitch of the body front on a holder. Work across the front, back, and other front to the V, and then back around again. Work even for two or three rows, then make a decrease at the neckline edge every two or three rows. The closer the spacing of the decreases, the wider the angle of the V. The wider the spacing of the decreases, the steeper the angle of the V. Continue decreasing at regular intervals until you've removed the number of stitches you plan to set aside for the neck back.

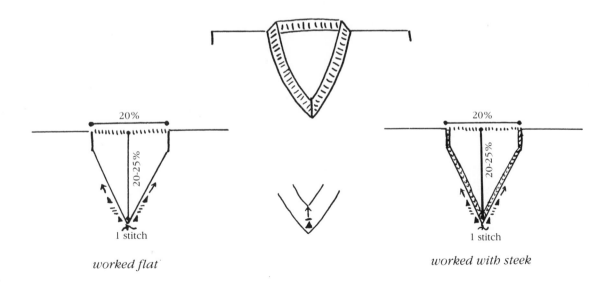

worked flat   worked with steek

To work the neckband for a wider V, begin at the shoulder edge with a circular needle, picking up one stitch at the end of *every* neckline row, knit across the stitch at the point of the V, then pick up at the end of every row up the other side and slip the neck back stitches onto the needle. Work in the round in ribbing, using a double decrease at the point of the V on every round.

If the neckline is a steeper V, work the ribbing in the same way, except in the 1½"-2" at the base of the V, pick up a stitch at the end of every four out of five rows instead of every row. With less space between the edges, you need fewer stitches to traverse the V. If your yarn is firmly spun and non-elastic, the wider angle V might require picking up four out of five rows in the last 1½"-2", while the steeper angle might require picking up three out of four. You might need to experiment a little to get a ribbing that doesn't gap at the point or draw the point upward.

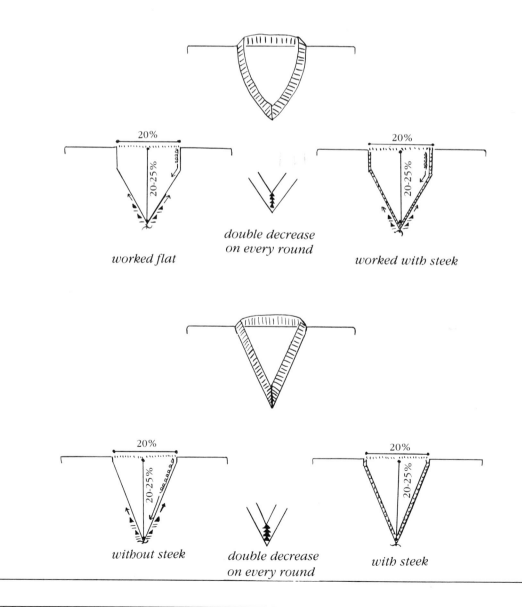

worked flat

double decrease
on every round

worked with steek

without steek

double decrease
on every round

with steek

Shawl collar. A shawl collar can be inserted into the V neck in place of a band. With the back neck stitches on a circular needle, work across the back neck stitches in ribbing or garter stitch. Pick up one stitch through the end of the row of the V neck edge. Turn you work, knit across the back neck stitches to the opposite side of the V neck, and again pick up one new stitch through the end of the first row. Continue in this manner, picking up one new stitch at each edge of every row as you work down sides of the V to the point. Then bind off around the entire collar. To allow the collar to lie flat, increase several stitches at each shoulder.

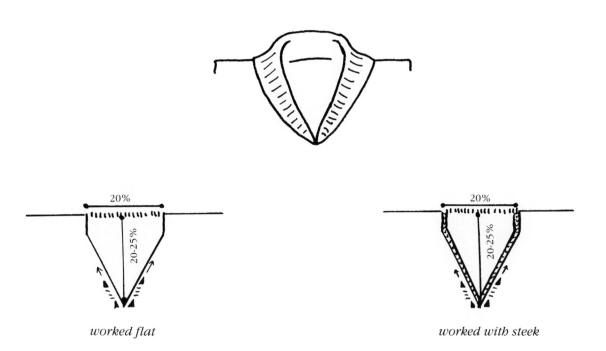

worked flat   worked with steek

Button neck closure. This is a short version of the cardigan closure, and is worked in the same manner, divided or steeked as you prefer. You can pick up the band and work around in one continuous piece, with a paired increase on each side of a center point stitch on every other row where the front band meets the corner of the neckline and the front edge. Or you can work a ribbing at the neck edge, with the button overlap worked separately. In either case, you can work the series of stitches at the base of the button overlap together with a perpendicular join. Work to the desired depth, placing the buttonholes in the appropriate positions as you go.

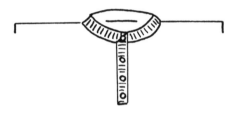

*ribbing worked continuously
around entire neck and placket*

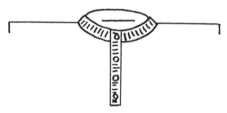

*ribbing at neck worked separately
from placket*

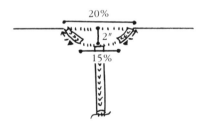

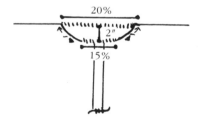

Traditional boat neck. Early boat necks were wide, straight openings, finished off with a short garter-stitch band worked in the round on the front and back. A tubular cord edging can also be used effectively; instead of picking up a stitch at each edge, incorporate the existing loops into the cord.

boat with narrow band   35-40%

Contemporary boat neck. Today's boat neck is also a flat opening, but it is often faced. Work the sweater up to the shoulder, and then keep working for the facing. Purl a row before starting the facing for a neat turn. If you've worked in the round with an armhole steek, close the steek off at this point and work the facing flat. When you've finished the facing, turn it under and sew each stitch to the sweater body. This eliminates having a bound-off edge which would make a ridge on the sweater. Sew the shoulder in as far as you wish, using a cross stitch through every purl stitch of the fold. The cross stitch should be on the inside of the shoulder seam, with only a bar joining purl stitch to purl stitch on the right side.

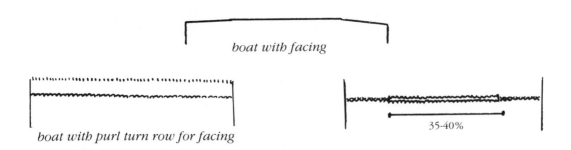

boat with facing

boat with purl turn row for facing   35-40%

Square neck. You can work a square neck by removing a group of stitches at the center front and center back at the desired depth, the front usually being deeper than the back. After joining the shoulders, pick up and work a band around the neck edge. For mitered corners, work double decreases at each corner on every other row.

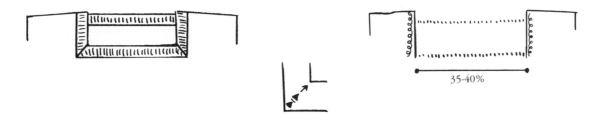

35-40%

Scoop neck. A scoop neck is a square neck with a curve in each corner. You can make a full curve by decreasing on every row, or a shallower curve by decreasing on every other row.

These are only the basic neck styles found on traditional folk sweaters, but they cover most of the range that you find even today. Experiment, combine techniques, try variations on a particular style; the only limiting factor is your imagination.

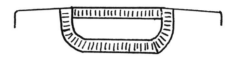

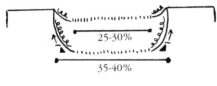

worked flat

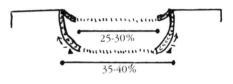

worked with steek

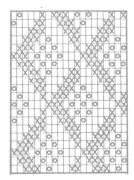

Color Stranded Sweaters

Color stranding dates back to the earliest known samples of knitting. This technique, often erroneously referred to as 'Fair Isle', involves working with two or more colors with the colors not in use carried loosely on the back of the fabric. Color stranding is most easily worked in the round with no more than two colors in any row.

In some parts of the world, knitters carry the yarn Continental style, with both yarns tensioned around the left forefinger (or left forefinger and middle finger). In other locales, the yarns are both carried in the right hand (one on the forefinger and one on the middle finger) in the English manner. Maintaining an even tension on both yarns tends to be more difficult this way. The simplest way to work color stranding is to use both hands—one yarn in the right hand, the other in the left. This technique is believed to have evolved among the Faroese; it's especially useful for working three colors simultaneously, holding two colors in one hand and one in the other. Developing the skill to work both Continental and English at the same time is worth the effort, but regardless of how you work, you need to become adept at controlling the tension of the strand running across the back of the fabric.

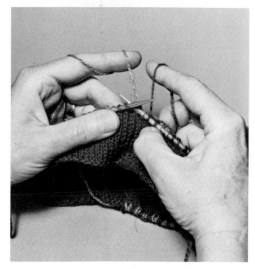

Color stranding with two colors simultaneously using both the English and Continental systems.

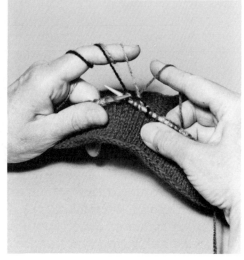

Color stranding with three colors; two are carried Continental, and one English style.

Using the two knitting systems, practice carrying dominant color in the right hand, and the less used one in the left; this will simplify working the more difficult designs. Don't change colors from one hand to the other once a row is in progress; this changes the way in which the yarns lie relative to one another across the back, and can cause a gap in the stitches on the surface. Practice working several rows of alternate stitches in two colors. As this becomes easy, space the color changes further apart. Beginners often pull the strand on the back of the fabric too tightly, which buckles it. The yarn not in use must be carried so that it lies across the back of the fabric smoothly, but not so loosely that it sags.

In most designs, color changes occur within a few stitches of each other. Should the design you're working require carrying the yarn over an extended distance (longer than, say, an inch), lock the strand into the back of the fabric so it won't snag in use. This is easy if you're working in the combined Continental-English manner and carrying the most frequently-used color (usually the background color) in the right hand. You need only to lift the left yarn up *above the right yarn* and knit the next couple of stitches with the right hand yarn. Then lower the left yarn to catch it a second time. *Do not* catch the yarn at *each* side of the stitch, because it will raise that stitch on the right side of the fabric, causing a bulge.

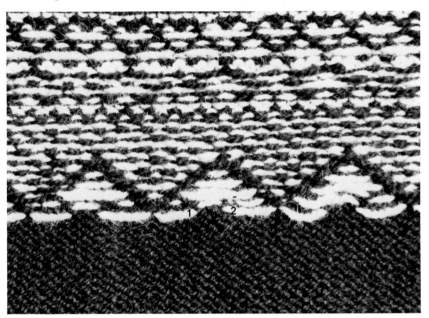

Back view of color stranded knitting. At #1, yarn is lifted to lock into fabric back. At #2, yarn is lowered to catch into fabric back.

If you're working back and forth in flat knitting, duplicate this same move on the purl rows; you'll find this a bit more difficult. But if you're timid about cutting into your knitting, or if you object to a folded cut edge, you must perfect this skill. On the purl side, lift the stranding yarn up and across the needle tip, make a couple of stitches, and then bring the yarn down, catching it a second time.

Most color stranded designs use only two colors per row, but some, especially those from Lapland, use three. To work such a design with three colors, carry the dominant color in the right hand and the other two in the left. Should the strands require securing in the back of the fabric, catch only one yarn at a time into the back of the stitches. Two strands caught together will push the stitch forward, visibly distorting the fabric surface.

Always work out your designs on graph paper; *never* try to work from written row-by-row instructions. You'll also find your designs easier to follow if the graph is done in the colors you'll be using instead of in symbols. Since the standard graph paper grid is square and knit stitches are not, many knitters prefer to work on 'knitter's graph paper', which is based on a proportion of five stitches to seven rows. When working your pattern, place your chart on a magnetic row keeper, as mentioned earlier.

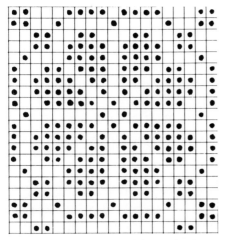

A dot chart on standard graph paper.

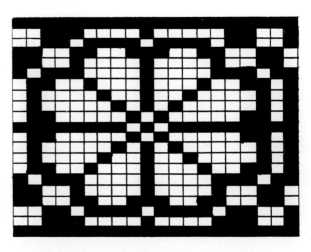

The same chart on knitter's graph paper.

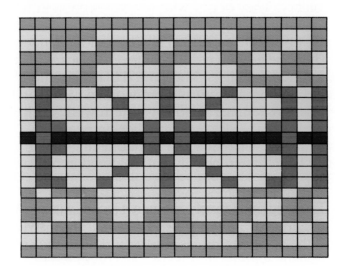

The same design worked out in several colors.

Let me repeat that color stranded patterns are much easier to work in the round. You'll need to use a steek (see page 39) or some other technique to bridge the openings that will need to be slashed. If you decide to work flat to avoid cutting, you will need to use a locked turning stitch (page 43) at your selvedges to secure every color that's been used in the row.

Color Stranded Sweaters of Norway

During the 19th century, beautiful color stranded sweaters and Norwegian knitting became synonymous. Color stranded designs, first worked in mittens, were quickly adapted to Norwegian sweaters. In this land of long, dark winters, color stranding doubled the fabric thickness, giving warmth while vividly enriching the garment with color and pattern. Early sweaters were knit from woolen or worsted handspun yarns, firmly spun for durability. Woolen sweaters offered greater potential for felting than worsted ones, and this was a common practice in some areas. The yarns were usually very firmly tensioned during knitting, resulting in a surface like richly embroidered fabric.

As mill spun yarns became available, most Norwegian sweaters were made of fine two-ply worsted yarns. The sweaters were knitted in the round with the armholes and neck cut and the sleeves worked from the shoulders down. Norwegian knitters today still work in the round and cut their work, but now they typically work the sleeves from the cuff to the shoulder and set them in; the neck opening is most often a boat style.

The *luskofte* is the most easily recognizable 'classic' Norwegian sweater. Originating about 1840 in the Setesdal valley, this classic man's garment came to worldwide attention as the national ski sweater at the Olympic games of the 1930's. During the German occupation in World War II it became an expression of national sentiment. The term *luskofte* means 'lice jacket', and refers to the speckled center ground in the sweater design. (This same spotted pattern was referred to as 'fleas' in Iceland—in both cases, possibly a reminder of bygone days!) These garments were knit of natural black and white yarn, often so fine that the firmly knitted patterns looked like embroidery. They began with a lower section in white which was covered by the large, high-waisted trousers typical of the era. Above this, a wide band of black stars or flowers were color stranded across the white ground. Then the ground color changed to black with several narrow bands of white geometric designs. The central black ground had the white flecks of 'lice', and the shoulder areas were worked in elaborate bands of small geometric designs. Similar bands of pattern were worked at both the upper and lower parts of the sleeves, with 'lice' in between. This dramatic garment was finished with cuffs and neck openings made of a woven and felted black fabric, often heavily embroidered in brilliant colors and closed with pewter clasps.

In the Fana region, a lovely woman's jacket was popular in the latter part of the 19th and early 20th centuries. This cardigan style was knit in the round and the openings cut, as was typical of all the color stranded work of Norway. Usually worked in blue or black with white, the lower edge had a diced or checkerboard band, shifting to horizontal stripes of alternating colors with specks of contrasting color in each stripe, and ending with a Nordic star design across the shoulder. The sleeves repeated the motifs of the body, although the wrist bands were usually in the star pattern rather than the checkerboard design of the waistband. The cut edges at the front and neck were bound with bands of woven fabric, as were the wrist bands. Closures were of pewter.

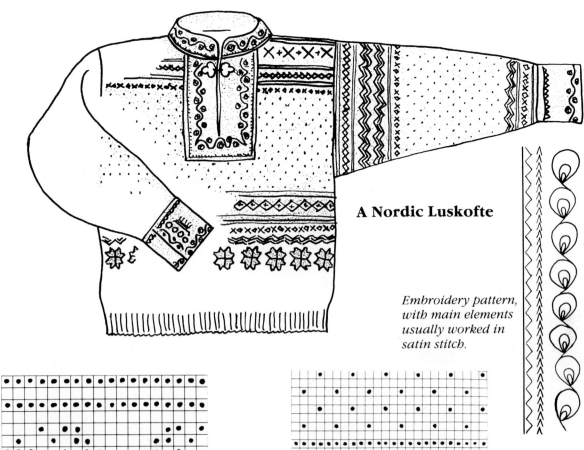

A Nordic Luskofte

Embroidery pattern, with main elements usually worked in satin stitch.

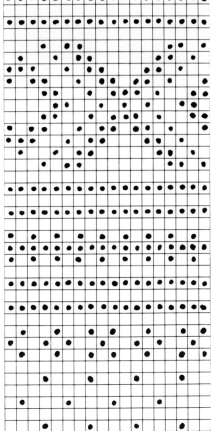

Pattern on upper part of sweater.

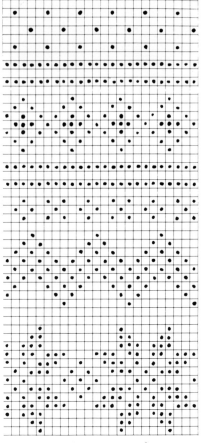

Pattern on lower part of sweater.

Modern Nordic, page 85

I chose a medium weight two-ply worsted yarn in the traditional deep blue and white with red accents for this sweater. The yarn measures 14 wraps per inch with 8 twists per inch; I used a size 6 needle for a gauge of 5½ stitches per inch. I knit it in the round, using the stitch and slash technique described in Plan 6. It has a boat neck with facing, page 75. I worked the sleeves from the cuffs up, with six rows at the top to cover the cut edges of the armholes on the inside. If you spin your own yarn, you can make a finer yarn for these last rows; they will cover the cut edge without adding much bulk to the seams.

Nordic Luskofte, page 80

I spun a firm two-ply semi-woolen spun yarn of natural black and white Merino, much like the yarns used traditionally for this sweater type. The yarns measured 16 wraps per inch with 14 twists per inch, and were knitted to a gauge of 6½ stitches per inch on number 4 needles. It follows Plan 6, with neck a button neck closure, page 74, adjusted for a wide fabric insert and collar. I knitted the sleeves from the cuffs up and bound them into the armhole so that the knitting direction would be the same as on the body. My fabric inserts are well-fulled woven fabric, although today many Nordic sweaters of this type use felt. The embroidery is worked in natural dyed handspun two-ply worsted type yarns.

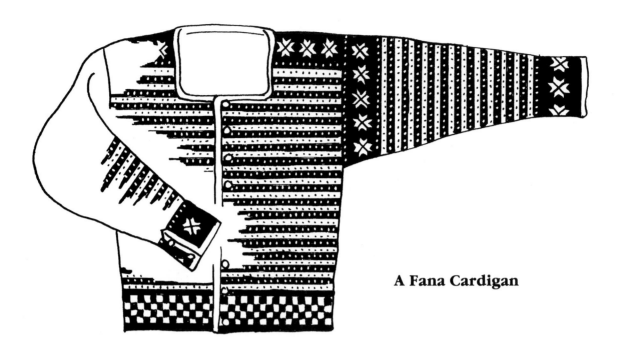

A Fana Cardigan

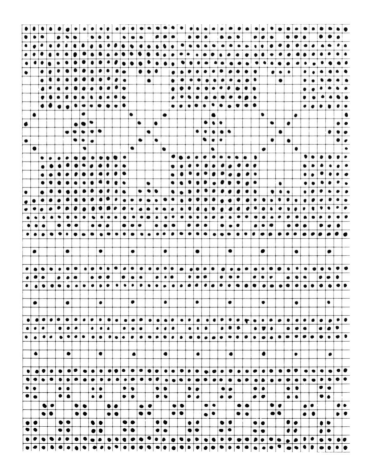

A turn-of-the-century coastal jersey incorporated the star pattern at the lower edge, across the shoulders, and at the upper arm, but instead of the lice pattern, it had an all-over design, frequently checkered. It was worked in the traditional manner, with one exception—a small half-gusset inserted at the underarm on the body, with these stitches removed to a holder while the rest of the garment was worked. Rather than carrying the gusset down the sleeve, the stitches were incorporated into the sleeve pattern itself. Rather than a fabric edge binding for the hem and wrist bands, the sweater often had a twisted edge cast-on in two colors followed by several rows of alternating color stitches to control the tendency to roll. The neckline was cut and edged with a decorative woven band.

The modern Nordic sweater, shown on pages 82 and 88, still retains the essence of the old designs, but it is greatly simplified. It is knit in the round with no provision for cutting the armholes. They are stitched by sewing machine and cut. The neckline is usually a boat neck. The sleeves are worked from wrist to shoulder with an extra four to six rows at the top to cover the cut edge of the body—a very neat finish on the inside, but one that adds bulk to the armhole seam. The color stranded portion is frequently limited to the shoulder area and the upper arm. A favorite color scheme is dark blue for the body of the sweater, with the design color stranded in white, and touched with a red band at the upper edges.

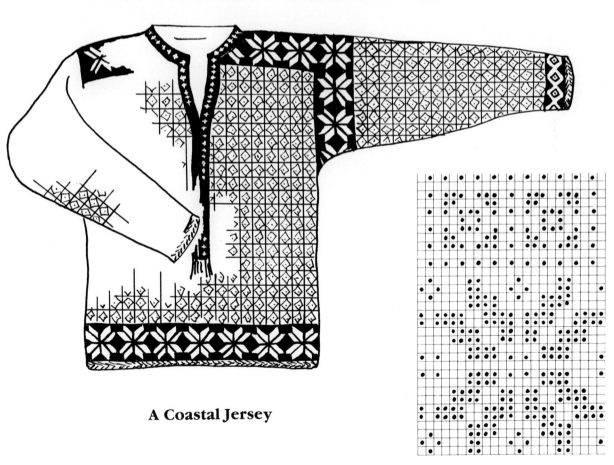

A Coastal Jersey

Swedish Bohus, page 98

I spun a two-ply worsted type yarn of wool and mohair for this sweater. The yarns measured 14 wraps per inch with 8 twists per inch, and were knitted to a gauge of 5½ stitches per inch on number 4 needles. If I had spun the yarn as a woolen, the sweater would have the fuzzier surface usually associated with mohair yarns. Both slipped and purled stitches accentuate the color stranded yoke pattern. I followed Plan 13, using five levels of wrapped turns to create short rows at the base of the yoke design. The subtle colors were inspired by autumn foliage against the rocks at Red Rocks Park near my home outside of Denver.

Icelandic Yoke, page 110

This sweater is of naturally colored authentic Icelandic lopi. I used two strands of unspun pencil roving, one from the outside and one from the inside of the plate. My needles were size 10, and the gauge 4 stitches per inch. The yarn is very fragile to knit, but it makes a sturdy sweater, thanks to the length of the fibers. This is an exceedingly lightweight but warm sweater. I followed Plan 12, using three levels of wrapped turns to create short rows at the base of the yoke to raise the back of the neck. The neck band is worked to twice the desired depth, turned under, and worked down stitch by stitch. The patterning is typical of this sweater type.

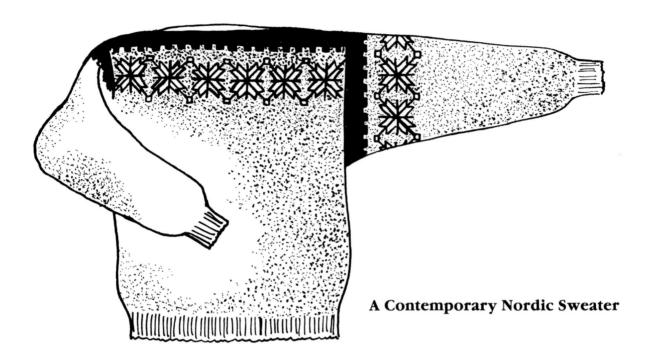

A Contemporary Nordic Sweater

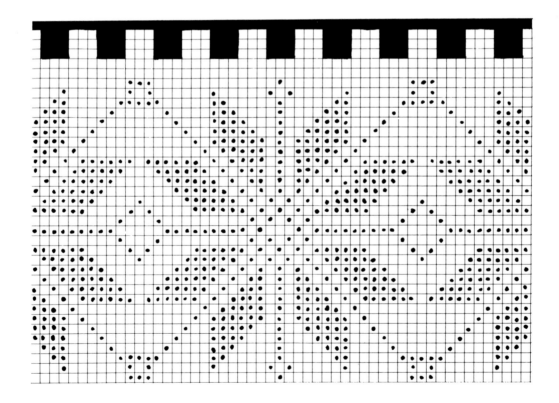

Color Stranded Sweaters of Sweden

Sweden is one of the few countries where the arrival of knitting can be dated. It was introduced in the mid-17th century by Magna Brita Crasaus, the wife of the newly appointed governor. Before this time, eyed-needle knitting variations were common, but not knitting as we know it today. The earliest sweaters were made of relatively coarse woolen yarns in one color.

Color stranded knitting became popular in the mid-1800s, especially in the Halland area, with none more distinctive than the Ullared jersey which was knit in red and black. This garment was knit very tightly in small diagonal patterns. Worn chiefly by loggers, it was designed to be both warm and wind-resistant. These sweaters shared design features with Danish blouses, although the patterns were interpreted with red and black color stranding rather than the one-color knit-purl brocading of Denmark.

The sweater often had a hip band in corrugated ribbing, with the stitches worked in alternating colors with all purl stitches in one color and all knit stitches in another. The side seams were decorated, which set off a center body panel of small diagonal patterning topped with a larger, bolder pattern across the shoulders. The center body section often contained a small rectangle (about 3″ × 5″) with the wearer's initials and the date knitted into the design. The sleeves were picked up at the shoulder and knit to the wrist, retaining the decorative seam treatment and diagonal design of the body. The wrist band was a different pattern, usually related to that of the shoulder. The edges of the neck opening and wrist bands were reinforced with a crochet edging.

The Delsbo jacket for men of the Halsingland area, a 19th century garment worked in red and green on a black or white background, was a short garment which began with a diced band of two colors. The main design began with smaller pattern bands and increased to very large ones. These designs were interrelated and developed into an over-all design, not just bands. They featured abrupt changes in color, making the vivid color contrasts even more striking. The Delsbo jacket was also structurally related to the Danish blouse; it often had a half-gusset and square neck faced with woven fabric, but omitted the side seam treatment in favor of carrying the design around the body. The sleeves were worked from the shoulders down, ending in a diced band at the cuff. The initials of the wearer and date of the knitting were sometimes worked into the bands of pattern rather than in a box as with the Ullared sweater.

The Bjarbo pattern was worked in red and blue on a cream ground. The sweaters often had a hip band worked in garter stitch with the purl rows of one color and the knit rows of another, red or blue against cream. The designs included all-over interlocking patterns, or patterns worked in bands. Their use of color changes was similar to that found on Fair Isle, with the center portion of the design in one color to contrast with the outer portions, but generally worked on the cream ground. These garments were knit in the round, and a system with two people working on the same garment simultaneously is known to have been practiced. One person would work at one side and the other would follow on the other side in such a way that each individual worked alternate rows on the body of the sweater.

Fair Isle Jersey, page 101

My yarn choice for this sweater was a two-ply worsted yarn, typical of those used in the Shetlands. Instead of the bright colors of early Fair Isle garments, I chose earth tones. I used the steeked jersey construction of Plan 3 with an underarm gusset, and the shaped crew neck on page 70. All the ribbed edges are are firm corrugated ribbing with a cable cast on. Two-color corrugated ribbing complements the bands of color stranded patterns. The shoulders are grafted, and the sleeves picked up and worked down to the cuff. Under close inspection you can see that the knit stitches in the sleeve are upside-down from those in the body, but this doesn't really affect the overall appearance and it does allow for a totally seamless garment.

Cowichan Shawl-Collar Pullover, page 116

I followed Plan 5 with neck variation #5 for a bold sweater reminis-
cent of the Pacific Northwest. (The collar is adapted according to the
Cowichan technique described on page 120.) I shaped the shoulders using
the short row technique and then bound them off together, which
avoided a lot of bulk.

The woolen yarn, spun from natural colored Corriedale fleece, is a
very bulky, firmly spun two-ply instead of the traditional single. It measures 5 wraps per inch with 6 twists per inch. My goal was to have greater
elasticity while retaining the robust quality of the traditional yarn. Because
my knitting gauge was very firm for this yarn (3 ½ stitches per inch), the
elastic yarn proved to be a problem; maintaining an even gauge while
stranding across the back was difficult. The Cowichan women must know
what they're doing, always working in a bulky single—they spend less
time spinning, and gain better knitting control!

Except for the changes in yarn and shoulder shaping, the design and
construction of this sweater is typical of the geometric Cowichan style,
with stripes in the ribbings and collar, and a dominant center band flanked
by two narrower bands—all in natural wool colors.

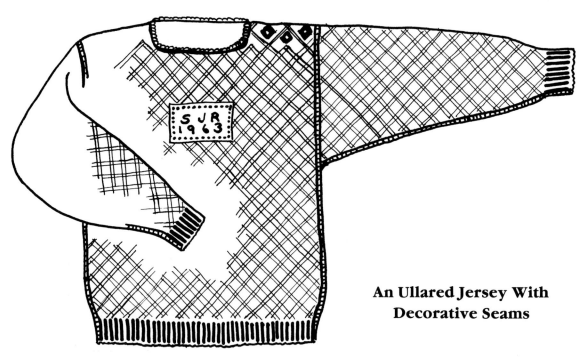

**An Ullared Jersey With
Decorative Seams**

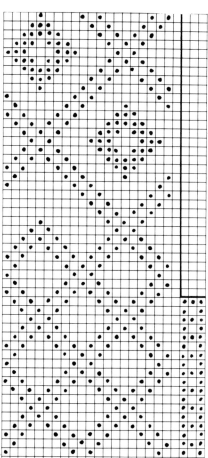

*underarm seam
stitches*

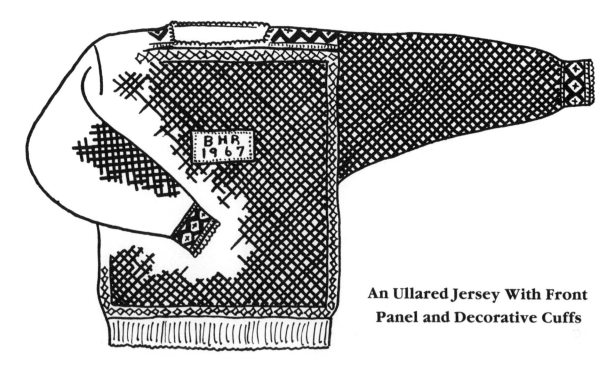

**An Ullared Jersey With Front
Panel and Decorative Cuffs**

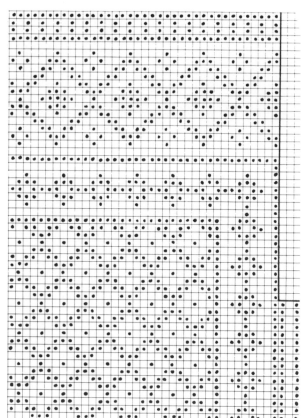

*underarm seam
stitches*

A Delsbo jacket

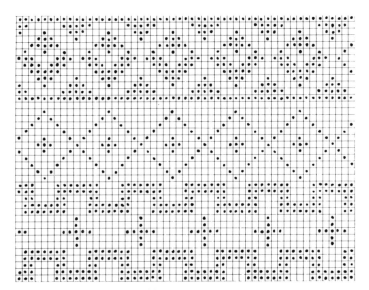

Upper pattern.

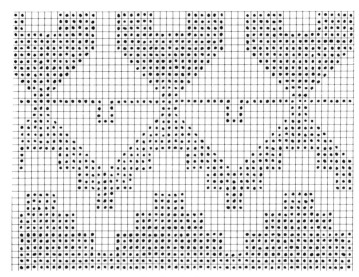

Lower pattern.

Center pattern.

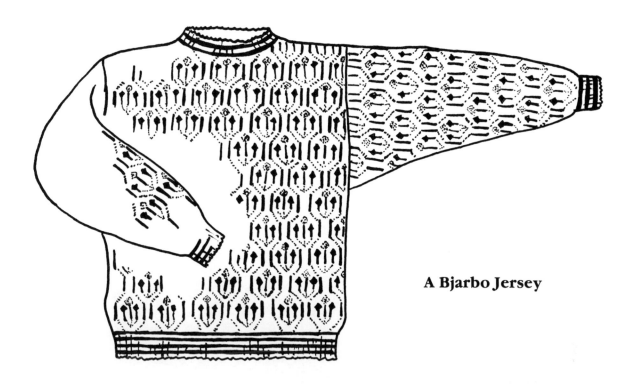

A Bjarbo Jersey

Since the pattern was always the same, this was not as difficult as it sounds.

A garment worn in some regions by both men and women was made with a woven fabric body and knit sleeves in elaborate color stranded designs. The woman's garment was often a snug-fitting bolero style while the man's was a loose jacket. In early examples, the body was usually a white woven fabric, with the sleeves color stranded in white and black; the entire garment was then dyed red or green, resulting in bright colored patterns against the black. The sleeves were worked in all-over color stranded patterns with deep cuffs of firmly knit bands or stripes of small patterns. The tension in these bands of alternating colors was pulled in tight to gather the cuff up and provide an elegant finish for the sleeve, which was often edged with fringe.

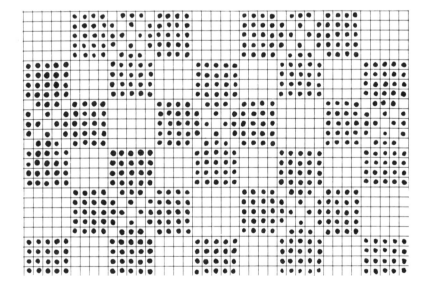

A Woman's Jacket With Knit Sleeves

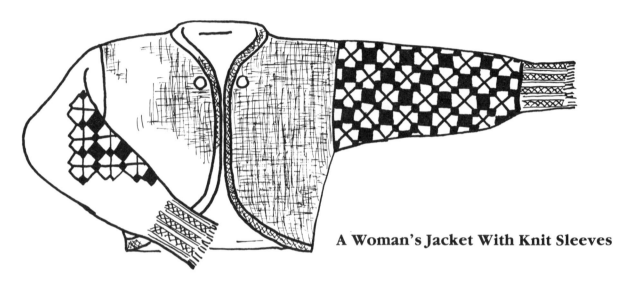

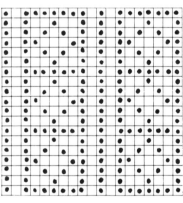

Cuff pattern.

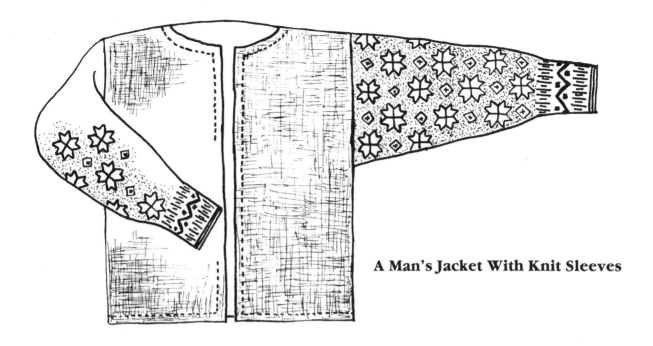

A Man's Jacket With Knit Sleeves

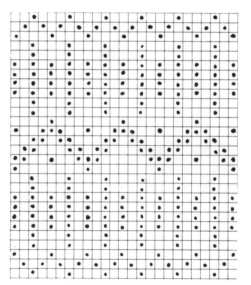

Cuff pattern.

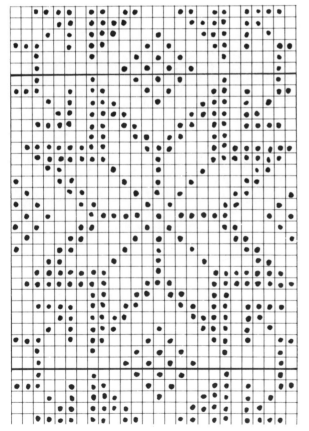

Sleeve pattern.

The Bohus sweater is a 20th century garment. In 1939, Emma Jacobsson organized the Bohus Knitting Cooperative in an attempt to alleviate the economic hardships of the times. Rather than continuing with strictly traditional designs, the group created a new direction in knitting. They designed seamless yoke sweaters worked in wool-angora blend yarns. Apparently, these were the first round-yoke designs, and their creation is credited to Ann-Lisa Mannheimer Lunn in the early 1940s. Although circular yoked sweaters are now used around the world, the Bohus sweaters were unique with their yokes combining many subtle shades of color. The designs were typically small interlocking bands, depending more on color shading than dominance of pattern. They incorporated subtle textural effects by means of purl stitches in portions of the design, while other portions used slipped stitches to carry the color from one row to the next. Their appeal lay in the subtlety of both color and pattern, combined with the luxuriously soft hand of the blended yarn.

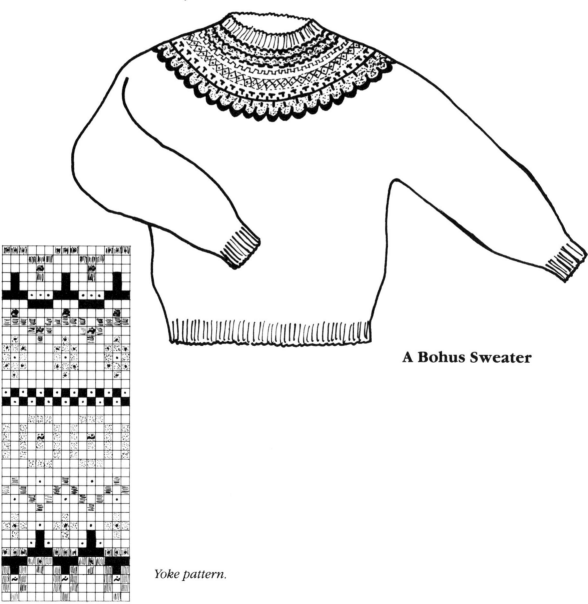

A Bohus Sweater

Yoke pattern.

Color Stranded Sweaters of Great Britain

Among the earliest of England's 'seaman's jerseys' was a garment knitted in the dales (highlands) for both sailors and miners. It was made of a heavy woolen handspun yarn called 'bump'. Hand knitting was vital to economic survival in the dales. Records show that local wool was carded, spun and knitted into jerseys for commercial trade by almost everyone, young and old. Handknitted hosiery for the gentry was also economically important, but it used worsted yarns not of local origin. (Stockings for local use were made of heavy woolen, not fine worsted, yarns.) There is no pictorial record of the 'seaman's jerseys', which were referred to as spotted or speckled 'frocks'—only diaries, letters and inventories which describe their appearance.

They were constructed of natural colored wools in two shades, light and dark, with stitches in alternate colors, both within the row and between rows. The bands at the edges were probably of corrugated ribbing—that is, with one color for the knit stitches and one for the purls, which resulted in a firm striped welt. These were seamless garments with the shoulders bound off together, armholes slashed, and sleeves picked up and worked down to the wrist bands.

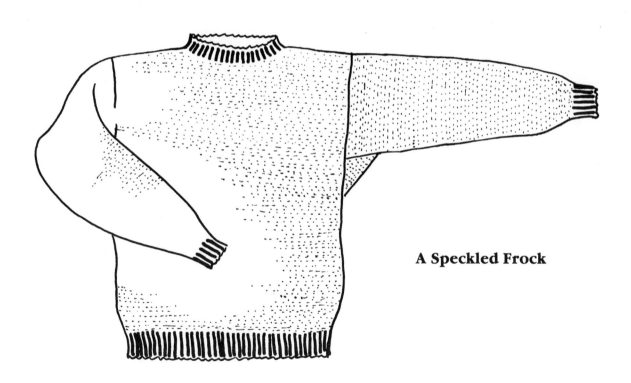

A Speckled Frock

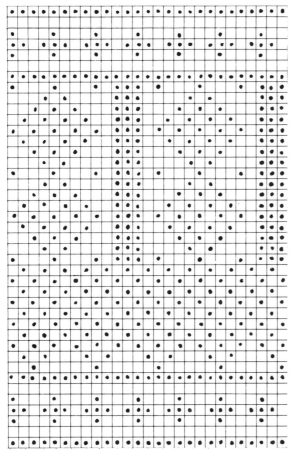

Pattern from speckled glove.

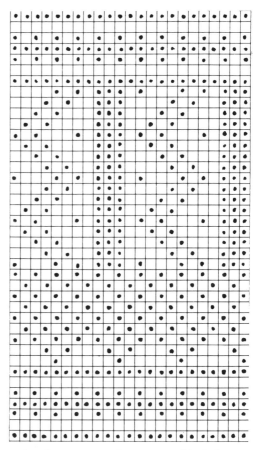

Another pattern from a speckled glove.

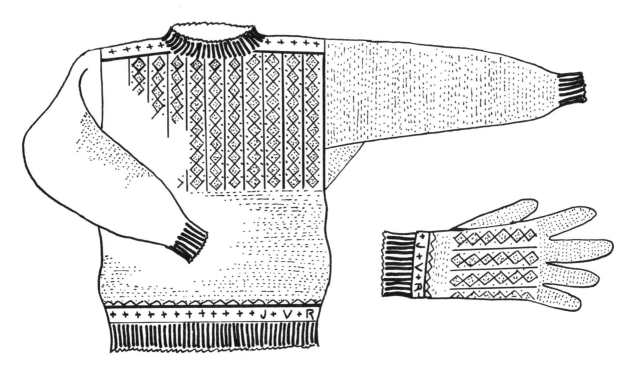

A Speckled Frock With Pattern Derived From Traditional Glove

By the mid-1800s, commercial production of the spotted frock in hand-spun woolen yarn had been replaced by the gansey-style garment with simple textured designs. But the long-standing tradition of working two colors in alternate stitches was not lost. Patterned gloves with speckles on the palms and fingers were popular, several of which have been preserved in museums. The gloves are very distinctive, with a small but elaborate pattern on the back of the hand and a patterned wrist band with the name of the owner. The wrist edge is finished with a fringe or a striped welt. These gloves were knit from finer worsted yarns which had become available from the early mills. It takes little imagination to transpose these beautiful patterns from gloves into sweaters, following the gansey shaping with a Scot's steek. There is no real evidence to indicate that these designs were actually used on sweaters, but it is in keeping with tradition that designs were often copied back and forth between sweaters, stockings and mittens. Furthermore, these gloves were being made when the earliest Fair Isle sweaters were knit in gansey shaping, so it is not difficult to imagine the designs in a color stranded sweater of that era.

The Shetland Islands (of which Fair Isle is best known), far to the north under the jurisdiction of Scotland, have a rich tradition of knitting, largely because of the fine wools produced by the native sheep. Early knitting of the 16th century consisted mostly of coarse stockings, but with the fall of the hosiery trade during the Victorian era, the islanders turned their knitting needles to other pursuits: lace shawls on Unst, and color stranded sweaters adapted from the traditional gansey shape on Fair Isle. The mostly symmetrical and geometric designs are usually worked in bands over an odd number of rows, which allows for symmetry. What is unique about the Fair Isle work is the use of color within the designs: only two colors are worked in any one row, but the ground color and pattern color shift within a motif, and pattern bands are often emphasized by the color changes. This color shifting within the bands makes the designs appear more complex than two-color stranding.

There are several stories about the origin of Fair Isle patterns. A romantic tale proposed by Eliza Edmondston in 1856 suggests that the patterns might be Spanish, learned from Spanish soldiers shipwrecked on the island in 1588—a highly improbable situation. On a small island barely able to sustain a native population of 50 inhabitants, the very real possibility of starvation must have been more on the minds of the populace than swapping knitting patterns with the 300 Spanish castaways. An even later embellishment of this tale discusses copying the patterns from the sweaters of the dead bodies washed ashore from the shipwreck. Records indicate, though, that the islanders simply wanted to be rid of these unwelcome intruders, and descendants of these island people vigorously repudiate this tale, in all its versions. According to the islanders, a seafaring native returned home with a woven patterned shawl, probably from the Baltics, which the women copied, adapting the designs to knitting. These designs evolved into more complex interpretations, and a 'new' folk art was born, probably around 1850. It is highly doubtful that these designs preceded the mid-19th century, as the oldest surviving pieces were worked in bright, vibrant color combinations not possible before 1840 when aniline dyes became readily

A Fair Isle Sweater in Gansey Construction

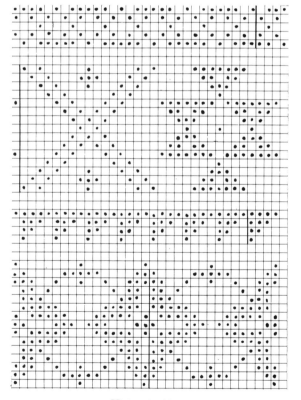

Upper pattern.

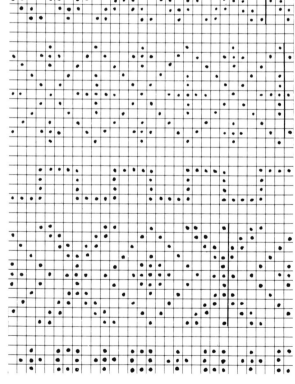

Lower pattern.

**A Fair Isle Shaped With Steeks
at Sleeve and Neck**

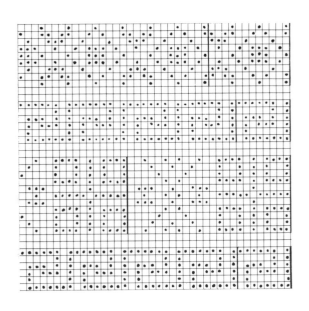

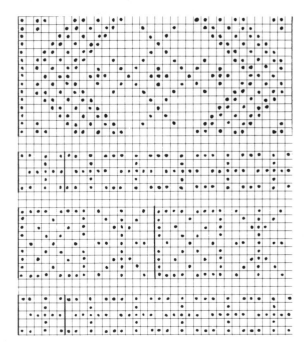

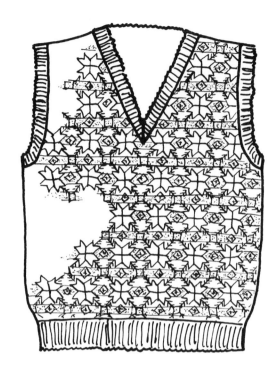

A Tesselated Vest

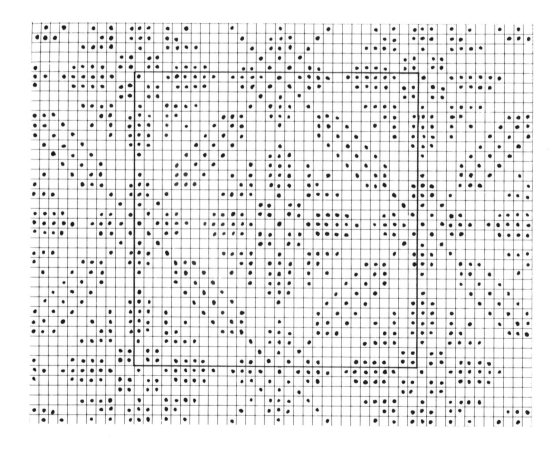

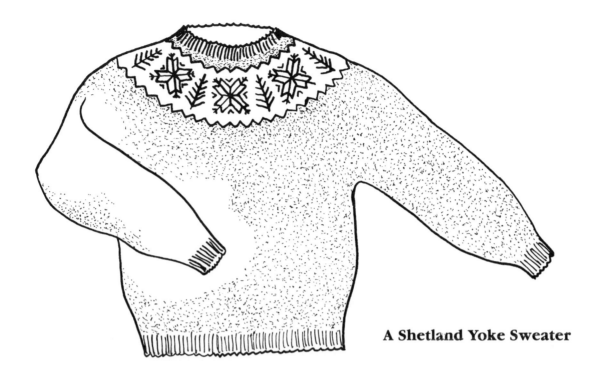

A Shetland Yoke Sweater

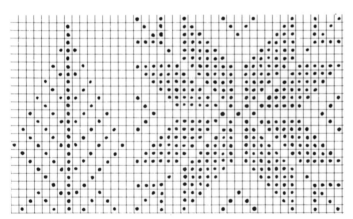

Yoke pattern.

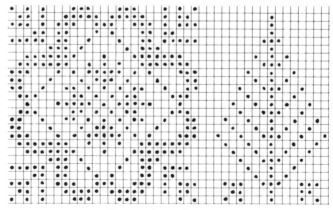

Alternative yoke pattern.

available to the islanders. By the early 20th century, natural fleece colors became popular for these designs.

The oldest of these sweaters follow the construction of the typical gansey, omitting the purl side seam to allow the designs to run continuously around the garment. A corrugated ribbing, often worked K2, P2, was used, above which the bands of design alternated between narrow and wide designs. The designs were not worked one in relation to the other, but relative to the total number of stitches in the circumference. This allowed the use of any repeat whose total stitches would evenly divide into the total. (If, in knitting this type of sweater, you choose a repeat that doesn't evenly divide into the total, make adjustments at *each* underarm, centering the design on both front and back.)

A gusset was worked at the underarm, but not separated from the main body of the sweater by a purl stitch. The gusset was usually worked in alternating colors instead of in the larger pattern motif, which eliminated long strands on the inside. Above the gusset, the stitches were removed to a holder, and the area closed with a steek which was also worked in alternating stitches. The shoulder seam was either grafted or bound off together on the inside. The steek was slashed, stitches picked up, and the sleeve worked down. The first band of pattern on the sleeve repeated the one located at the center of the armhole, and the remaining bands repeated in order down the sleeve. Interestingly though the knitters of the Shetlands worked in the round, they didn't use multiple needles as in most other areas. They used three long needles; all the front stitches were on one, the back stitches on another, and the third was the working needle.

When shaping became more popular in the 20th century, the gusset was omitted; a set of platform stitches was removed at the base of the armhole, the opening steeked, and the armhole shaped with a series of decreases on each side of the steek. Often a V neck was used, again with the opening steeked and decreases worked on each side of the steek.

Today, many of the designs are made up of all-over interlocking motifs rather than the traditional bands. But the appearance of bands is still maintained by the changing the colors of the ground stitches within the designs. This particular variation is especially popular for sleeveless vests. The practice was, and still is today, to block these sweaters when the knitting is complete. The sweater is completely wetted and stretched on an adjustable frame which holds the sweater taut while it sits to dry in the sun. This evens any variations in tension on the stranding yarns, resulting in a very smooth surface.

A further evolution of the Fair Isle design is the Shetland yoke sweater, a garment that has grown more popular in the last 25 years. Even though the design is Fair Isle in origin, to call the garment a Fair Isle sweater is inaccurate. This style is a product of all the Shetland islands, a simplification adapted from the commercially successful Fair Isle sweaters. The Shetland yoke can be worked in several small pattern bands, with the decreases set between the bands. More typically, the yoke has one pattern band with decreases incorporated between design elements. This technique is simplified by the use of a square pattern element alternating with a triangular one; the regular rounds of decreases at the edges of the squares simultaneously taper the edges of the triangles.

Color Stranded Sweaters of Iceland

The sheep of Iceland are unique to this north Atlantic island, brought by the early Viking settlers in the 9th and 10th centuries. Adapting to the climatic conditions, the sheep evolved a fleece consisting of two different coats: the outer coat of long, glossy hairs, ranging from 12″ to 19″ in length, offers protection from wind, rain and snow. The shorter inner coat of fine, soft, fluffy fleece fills the space between the long outer hairs, providing excellent insulation. A yarn spun from this two-part coat is similar to one blended of mohair and Merino. Softly spun in a bulky weight, the yarn is exceedingly lightweight and traps a lot of insulating air.

Handknitting has long been a tradition in Iceland; it probably came to them from the Dutch in the 1600s. Records show the craft to have been an important activity; a jersey dates back to around 1700, and early manuscripts show simple color stranded designs charted on graph paper. The working man's sweater, called an 'Icelander', was a bulky garment knit in two, or occasionally three, natural wool colors. It was a very simple garment both in shape and patterning, with small geometric designs closely spaced. Made of heavy woolen yarn, this was possibly the earliest of the "bulky" sweaters, with even greater warmth provided by the color stranding, which doubled the fabric while making it firm and inelastic. In addition, many 'Icelanders' were felted to provide even more resistance to the elements.

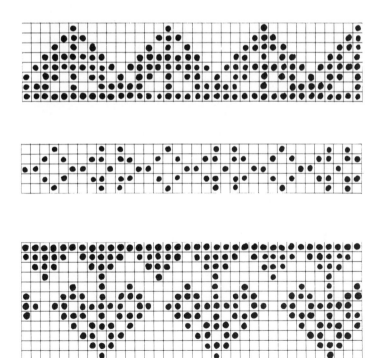

Knitted border patterns from 1776 manuscript.

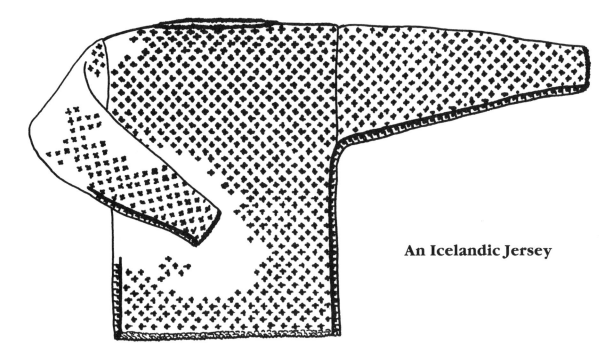

An Icelandic Jersey

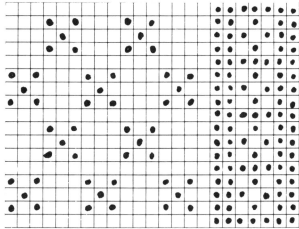

An Icelandic pattern with colors reversed in the seams.

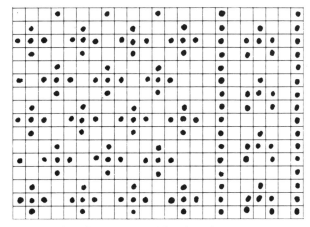

An Icelandic pattern with related seam pattern.

The example shown dates to the late 1800s or early 1900s. Little attention was given to edge treatments; the lower edge at the hips was worked in a twisted edge cast-on in two colors, and the design started after several twisted two-strand rows. A design feature often found on this type of sweater is a five- to seven-stitch side seam panel at the under arms which was often given emphasis by being worked in colors the reverse of those in the body of the sweater, or by outlining the panel with the pattern yarn. The design motif in the panel might be identical to that in the rest of the garment, or if the panel were outlined, it might be a slightly different but related design. To maintain the continuity of the design from body to sleeve, the panel stitches were removed at the underarm and the armhole closed with a steek (or with a locked stitch incorporating both colors of the row). The neck opening, as in this example, was a straight boat neck, with the edge bound off and allowed to roll slightly. The shoulder can be bound off together or grafted. Traditionally, the sleeves were picked up at the armhole and worked to the wrist, with the seam panel design maintained and decreases on each side of it for sleeve shaping. There is no cuff; the edge is bound off and allowed to roll. To control the tendency to roll, replace the pattern with a few row of 'fleas'—the traditional Icelandic term for alternating stitches of two colors.

When textile manufacture was first industrialized in Iceland, the wool was often made into plates of roving at the mill and returned to the farmer to be spun at home. The Icelandic term for this roving is *lopi*; it was not used for knitting until 1920, when Elin Guomundsdottir Snaeholm, rather than taking the time to spin the yarn, attempted to knit directly from the lopi. She successfully created a lopi scarf on a knitting frame; her experiments were published, and by 1923, the practice had begun to spread so that today, lopi is synonymous with the soft roving-type yarns of Iceland.

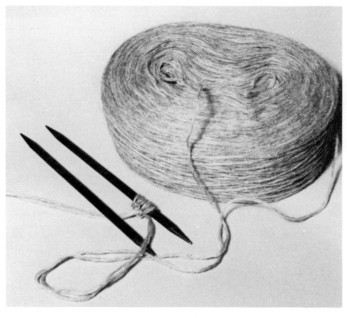

Unspun lopi plate from Iceland.

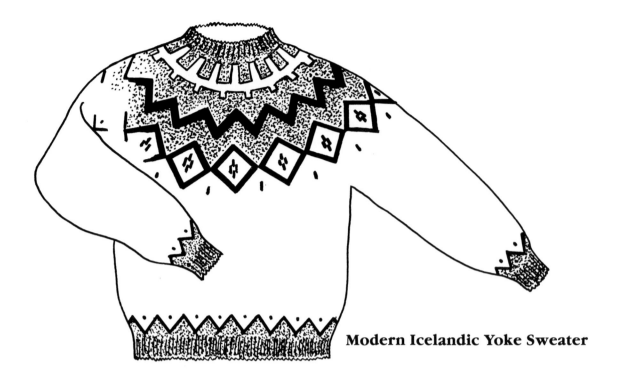

Modern Icelandic Yoke Sweater

Icelandic yoke in bands with decreases occuring between pattern motifs.

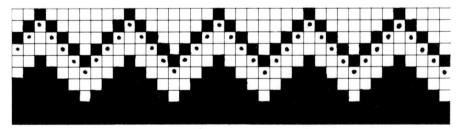

Hip and cuff pattern.

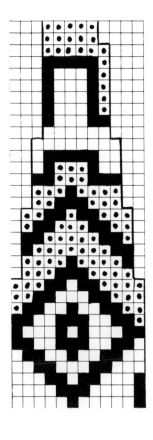

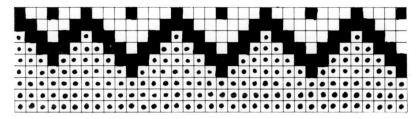

*Interlocking pattern for
an Icelandic
yoke, with decreases
incorporated into
the pattern.*

Hip and cuff pattern.

The use of lopi in handknit sweaters became popular during World War II, and today, the round yoke design in natural colored lopi yarns is *the* Icelandic sweater. Interestingly, the designs for this style are decidedly Scandinavian in influence; the round yoke treatment is clearly an imported idea. In 1957, the Alafoss Spinning Mill began to manufacture the unspun yarns on a commercial scale, catapulting the handknitting of lopi sweaters into economic importance. Though handknitting is no longer economic in most cultures, this lofty yarn works up quickly enough to make the handwork profitable. With it, knitting as a cottage industry figures materially in the Icelandic economy. In addition to lopi, one- and two-ply woolen yarns are also very popular among handknitters in Iceland.

Seamless pullovers are knit in the round, with a full yoke pattern worked in two or more natural colors. The circular yoke design is often complemented by narrower bands at the hip and wrists. Cardigans are worked flat, as the slashing technique doesn't work well on such a fragile and bulky yarn. A turned lock stitch at the center front is recommended.

Incidentally, the Icelandic yarn marketed in the United States for handknitting has more twist inserted than the yarn available in Iceland. For domestic use, the yarn is sold as a one-ply plate—a flat, round roll of roving. To create a bulky yarn, the knitter uses the ends from the inside and outside of the plate together; they wrap loosely together as they unwind. Very lightweight garments can be made by working with a single roving from the plate.

Color Stranded Sweaters of the Faeroe Islands

The term 'faeroe' means sheep, and sheep have truly been important in the life of the Faeroese. Sheep were first brought to the islands by Irish monks, but they died out in the 18th century and were replaced with sheep imported from Shetland. The wool was gathered by hand plucking (the local term is 'skubbering'), then was both spun and knit in the grease. The finished garment was scoured and felted simultaneously. In early times on festive occasions, men wore a jacket cut and tailored from a felted knit fabric. The women also wore felted knit garments; these were usually short sleeved, cut down the front, and laced with a decorative chain. Many of these early garments were so heavily felted that the knitted structure was almost impossible to see.

The Faeroe jersey is closely related to the old 'Icelander', both in design and construction. The patterns are small geometric shapes, often worked in narrow bands with ground and pattern color alternating. Luckily, the old designs were recorded in the early 1900s and labeled with their traditional names. They appeared as samplers in an exhibition in Copenhagen and have since been published. The yarn used in these sweaters was a fairly bulky woolen yarn, often felted after knitting to increase resistance to wind and cold.

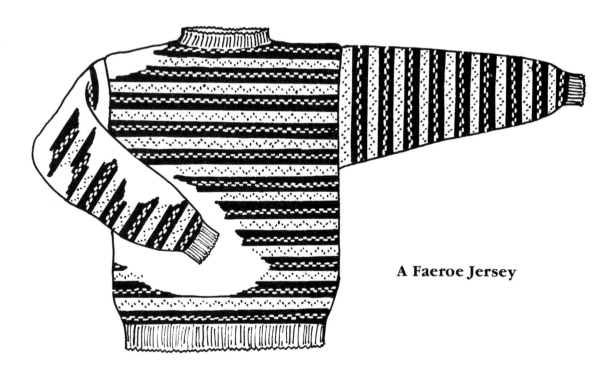

A Faeroe Jersey

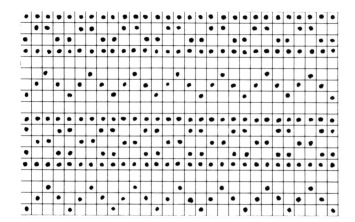

Pattern for striped Faeroe jersey.

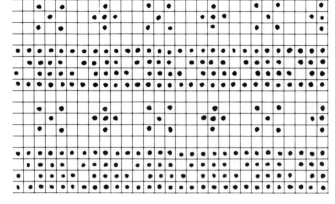

Alternative pattern for a striped Faeroe jersey.

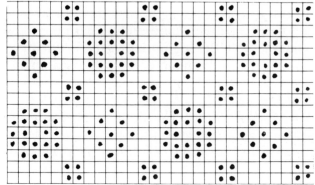

Overall patterns for Faeroe jerseys.

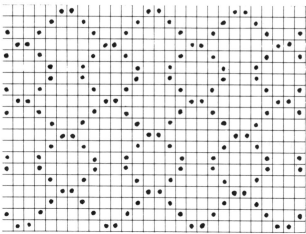

Color Stranded Knitting of Lapland

Lapland lies within the Arctic Circle, extending across the northern areas of Norway, Sweden, Finland, and into Russia. The Lapps were nomads who roamed the northernmost frontiers herding reindeer; even in the southernmost reaches of their wanderings, they had to survive long, dark, bitterly cold winters. Today, Lapps travel much less than before, and their lives are greatly eased by snowmobiles, yet their environment has changed little. Living in this austere region of the world, they have developed a love of bright primary colors, as shown in their traditional garments heavily embossed with brilliant embroidery. Although not great knitters, they do contribute mittens of a style not found in other countries of northern Europe. They use simple patterns boldly worked in red and blue on a cream ground, with touches of yellow and pale blue. They often use more than two colors in a row. The mitten cuffs are usually worked in cable purl twist in two colors accompanying a zig-zag pattern.

Although not traditionally used in sweaters, the Lapps' charming designs can be adapted into a loosely fitting tunic shaped like their woven and embroidered garments. Working from a two color cast-on, just as you'd find in the Lapp mittens, followed by double purl twist and a band of patterned color stranding, work the body of the garment in the main color. Their woven tunics are usually red, but a sweater could be worked in primary colors on a cream ground like the mittens. Working in the round to the underarm, either divide the work or steek the armhole above three to five platform stitches, and at the same time, remove a series of stitches to accommodate a neckband, steeking the center front opening.

Continue to work in the main color until you've completed about two-thirds of the armhole depth; then work a pattern band ending with the double purl twist in two colors to resemble the seam that would normally appear at the yoke front. Finish the piece in the main color while shaping the neck as necessary to accommodate the neckband, and graft the shoulders. Pick up the sleeve stitches at the armhole, working the double purl twist in two colors followed by a band of pattern. Continue in the main color, decreasing at the underarm at regular intervals until the sleeve is long enough, finishing with a pattern band and several rows of double purl twist before binding off.

To complete the neck, pick up stitches along the left front, across the back of the neck, and down the right front. Then, working a K2tog or SSK as necessary, work into body stitch at the end of each row to knit the band and finish the front opening simultaneously. Centering a band of pattern into the available neck stitches, work a color stranded band, ending with a few rows of double purl twist immediately before the bind-off row. Add pewter clasps as a finishing touch on this interpretation of a Lapp design.

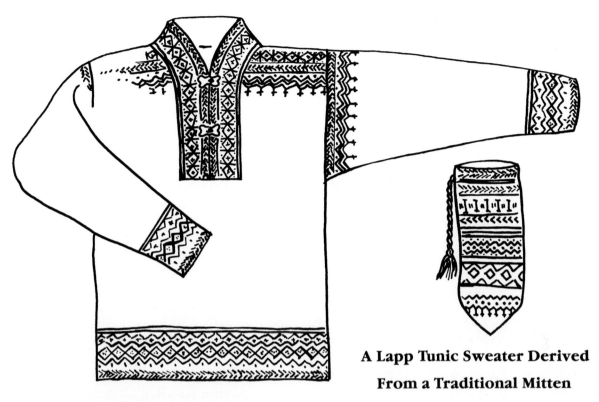

A Lapp Tunic Sweater Derived From a Traditional Mitten

Upper pattern.

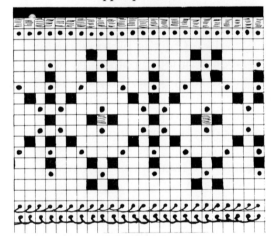

Neck band.

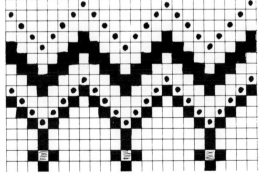

Upper sleeve.

Lower pattern.

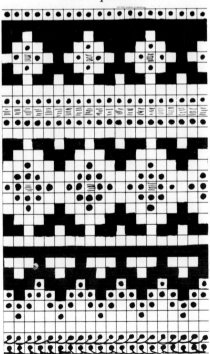

Color Stranded Cowichan Sweaters of Canada

The only true folk sweaters of North America are those of the Cowichan Indians—garments widely copied, but seldom equalled. These particular sweaters are unique in that, even today, they are made exclusively of hand-spun yarns. Furthermore, they are always handknit, as knitting machines can neither handle the heavy yarns nor duplicate the tightly knit fabric of authentic Cowichan sweaters.

In 1864, the Sisters of St. Ann opened an Indian school in the Cowichan Valley of Vancouver Island, and included knitting in their course of study. The native women, already skilled in handspinning, first used their bulky yarns for stockings, mittens, and caps. Jerimina Colvin, a Scottish settler who emigrated to Canada in 1885, is credited with showing these women how to apply their knitting skills to making sweaters—turtle necks in one color. In time, these knitters began to embellish their sweaters with the geometric designs of their basketry, using the natural colored wools of local sheep in color stranding techniques—and in so doing, their acquired craft became a true folk art. The Cowichans further modified their sweaters to include an unusual shawl collar, and they began to incorporate highly stylized representational motifs adapted from other sources.

The early geometric designs were most often worked in five horizontal bands. A wide center band dominates the body of the sweater and is repeated on the upper arms. Narrower pattern bands are repeated on both sides of the center band, with the first and fifth bands being stripes incorporated into the hip ribbing and the collar. With the use of non-geometric designs such as representations of flora and fauna from non-Indian sources like embroidery books, the center band is replaced by the pictorial design, then bounded on one or both sides by smaller geometric pattern bands, retaining the stripes as before. The sleeves, rather than using the pictorial motifs, usually use a wide band of geometric design like the center band of the all-geometric sweaters. The sweaters are often done in two natural colors, although a third color is sometimes added by changing the ground color within the geometric bands.

The yarns for authentic Cowichan sweaters are handspun, the earliest being spun on large handspindles, and today spun on specially adapted spinning wheels known as 'bulk' or 'Indian head' spinners. The Cowichans were the first to adapt the traditional spinning wheel to accommodate bulky yarns, using treadle sewing machine bases cast aside by the Anglo population in favor of electric sewing machines. A modification they made to the treadle base is today copied and produced for handspinners working in bulky designer-type yarns. The yarns produced by the Cowichan women are thick, one-ply roving-type yarns with a fairly firm twist—a yarn that is firm and sturdy rather than light and lofty. The yarn is firmly knit into an extremely hardwearing, solid fabric; a typical Cowichan knitter uses a size 7-9 needle for yarn that the typical American knitter would work up on size 13-15.

The pullover sweater is knit in the round to the underarm where a few stitches are added for ease. The work is divided, and the back worked to the shoulders. The front is further divided into two equal sections, and a V neck formed as it is worked up. The shoulders are shaped by binding off a

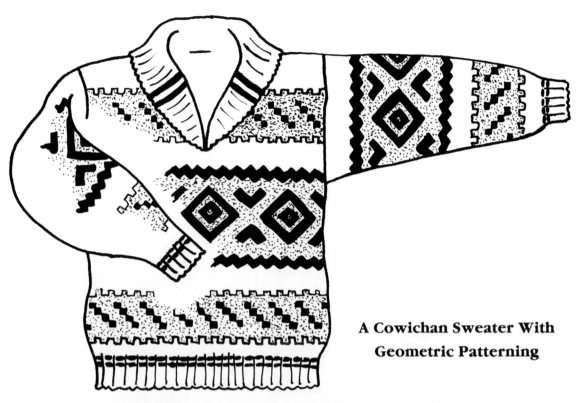

**A Cowichan Sweater With
Geometric Patterning**

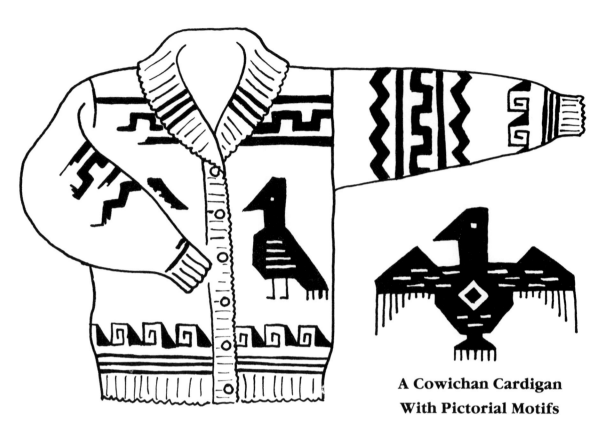

A Cowichan Cardigan
With Pictorial Motifs

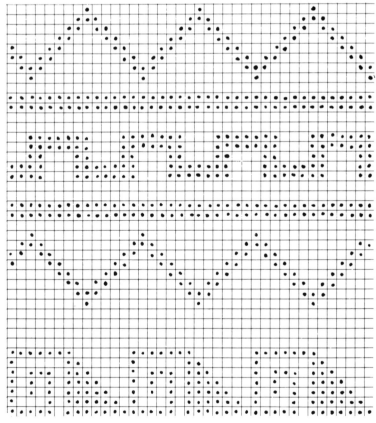

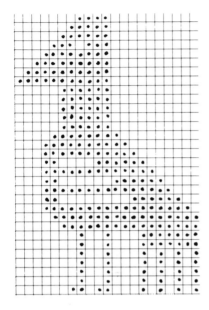

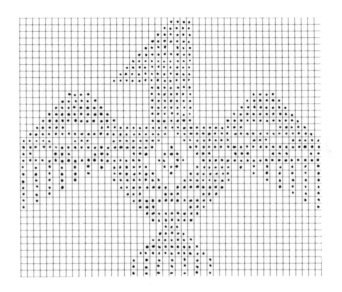

third of the stitches at the sleeve edge at the beginning of each row. An alternate, and more desirable method, is to use the short row technique described on page 59, binding off the front and back together and thus eliminating much of the seam bulk of the traditional technique. The sleeves are then picked up and worked to the wrist.

The shawl collar is rather unusual in that the back of the collar is most often knit separately from the two fronts. After the shoulders have been joined, the center back neck stitches are worked back and forth on two needles in garter stitch, increasing by one stitch at the beginning of each row until the appropriate collar depth has been reached. The stitches are then bound off. Stitches are picked up along each side edge of the collar back and worked in garter stitch. The collar front is thus worked separately on each side, with the last stitch of the row knitted into the end of each row of the neck edge of the sweater front, simultaneously knitting the collar and attaching it to the sweater. When the number of stitches on the needle is equal to the number of rows remaining on the neck edge, the collar is decreased by one stitch in every row, shaping the collar as the work progresses down to nothing at the point of the V. An alternate construction is to work the whole collar at once in garter stitch, working across the back neck stitches, picking up a new stitch at each end of the row, continuing down and around the V neck, binding off all the collar stitches at once. To insure enough fullness for the collar to lie smoothly, additional stitches may be necessary in the shoulder seam area.

The early sweaters were pullovers, but today, many are cardigans. On these, the body is worked back and forth and the sleeves in the round, with the collar adapted for a button overlap. When a representational design is used, the cardigan front is handled as two separate units, each side a mirror image of the other. The design itself might be an adaptation of the design on the back of the garment or a complimentary, but totally different, design.

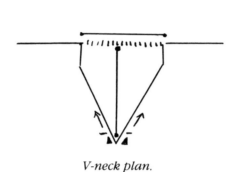

V-neck plan.

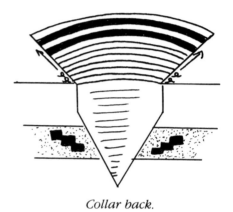

Collar back.

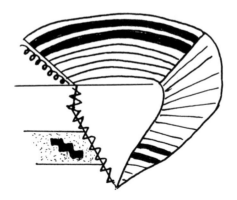

The collar side fronts in progress.

The Cowichan shawl collar.

Many commercial adaptations of the Cowichan sweaters are available today, both as patterns and as garments, more often than not in a raglan style of commercially-produced lofty six-ply yarn. The true Cowichan is always knit of a firm one-ply handspun, firmly tensioned for a sturdy fabric, and always in the square shaping with sleeves picked up and knit down to the wrist. Authentic, well-made Cowichan sweaters are often sought as collector's items, especially popular in Japan.

Color Stranding American Folk Art Designs

Although in the United States we lack a distinctively national knitting tradition, we have an abundance of folk art motifs that are readily adapted to color stranded knitting. In recent years, a folk art look has emerged using stylized figures in bands of color stranded patterns, the figures copied from other folk art media, with hearts, birds and tulips predominating. The most common style seems to be a boxy vest with little or no shaping, often very loosely fitted. A deep armhole is finished with a wide band of ribbing which results in a loose shoulder line, while the neck is often a straight boat style or a widely fitting crew.

American "Folk Art" Sweater

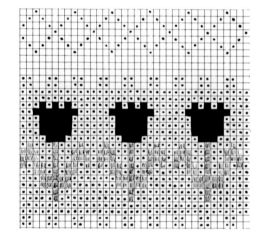

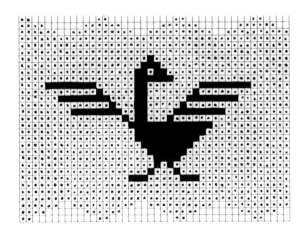

Another motif frequently cropping up, is various renditions of sheep. The sheep might be around the yoke of the garment, or on the body of a typical jersey. This particular style is most frequently seen among handspinners who especially love these wooly creatures, although it seems to be popular among the general population also.

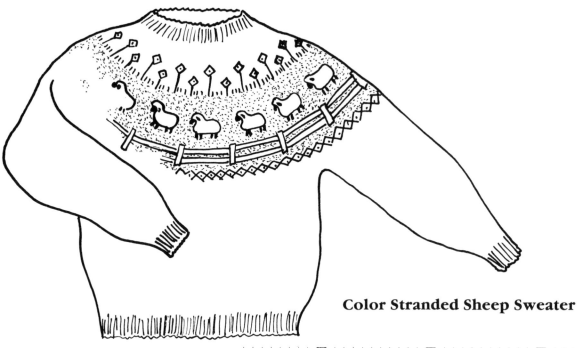

Color Stranded Sheep Sweater

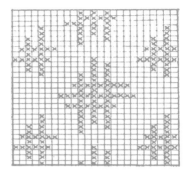

Textured Sweaters

Textured patterns range in difficulty from very simple knit-purl sequences through the basic traveling stitch patterns to complex embossed designs. The work itself is relatively easy to master, but reading the instructions can be a mind-boggling experience! Charting the designs on graph paper with a system of symbols gives an easy-to-follow visual representation of the design.

When diagramming textured designs, use standard graph paper, preferably four squares to the inch, because the symbols are easier to read than on knitter's graph paper. The chart here shows just the basic moves, as most pattern knitting is little more than variations of knit and purl stitches. In situations requiring variations, you can adapt the symbols for that particular use. Here's how to adapt the '*ℓ*' (make one raised increase); if the pattern calls for a bar increase (knit one through the front and back loop of the stitch), you can add a bar to the symbol to read '*ℓ*'. Or, the same '*ℓ*' increase can be adapted to read '*ℓ*' to signify a raised purl increase.

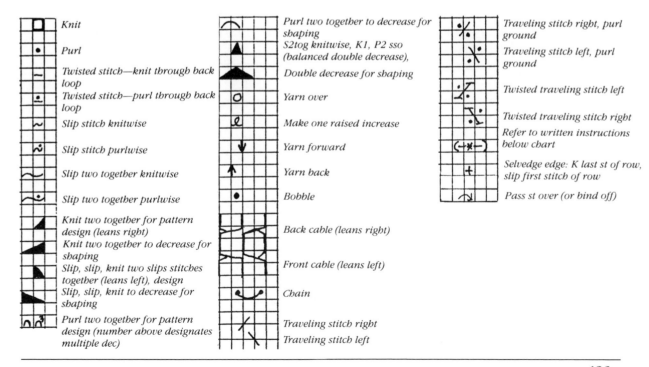

	Knit
•	Purl
−	Twisted stitch—knit through back loop
•	Twisted stitch—purl through back loop
~	Slip stitch knitwise
~	Slip stitch purlwise
~	Slip two together knitwise
~	Slip two together purlwise
	Knit two together for pattern design (leans right)
	Knit two together to decrease for shaping
	Slip, slip, knit two slips stitches together (leans left), design
	Slip, slip, knit to decrease for shaping
	Purl two together for pattern design (number above designates multiple dec)
	Purl two together to decrease for shaping
▲	S2tog knitwise, K1, P2 sso (balanced double decrease), Double decrease for shaping
O	Yarn over
ℓ	Make one raised increase
↓	Yarn forward
↑	Yarn back
•	Bobble
	Back cable (leans right)
	Front cable (leans left)
	Chain
	Traveling stitch right
	Traveling stitch left
	Traveling stitch right, purl ground
	Traveling stitch left, purl ground
	Twisted traveling stitch left
	Twisted traveling stitch right
(−*−)	Refer to written instructions below chart
+	Selvedge edge: K last st of row, slip first stitch of row
	Pass st over (or bind off)

Written directions for textured designs are usually given for flat knitting. If you're working in the round, you'll need to transcribe the directions accordingly, making a graphic representation of the right side of the fabric. To do this easily, transcribe all the right side rows first, then fill in the wrong side rows, reversing them. In most patterns the correct notation for these reverse rows becomes obvious once you've established the pattern.

If you plan to work flat, you can record the pattern as you work, with alternate rows showing the wrong side of the fabric. To denote whether the work is recorded for circular or flat knitting, number all the rows on the right side of the chart. For flat knitting, number odd rows on the right and even rows on the left. A word of caution: when transcribing a pattern from written instructions, always check to see if the pattern begins on the right or wrong side of the fabric. If the directions indicate the first row is a wrong side row, number the odd rows on the left and the even ones on the right.

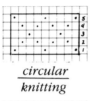

circular knitting

flat knitting

Since the circular chart is a better visual representation of the work, many knitters prefer to work from this type of chart even when working back and forth; in doing so, they remember to work each stitch in reverse, working knits as purls and purls as knits.

Simple Knit-Purl Designs

Often referred to as 'damask' and 'brocade', purl designs on a stockinette ground have been used for pattern knitting for a long time. The earliest use of pattern on garments for the upper classes was in silk frocks with elaborate knit-purl motifs, and these were probably first copied by the common folk in Denmark for their damask blouses. The designs depend on subtle surface texture rather than bold relief. Sometimes the designs were made to stand out more prominently by alternating single purl and knit stitches (what we call seed stitch) within the sections of the pattern. The knit stitch *below* each purl of the seed stitch was often worked through the back loop to twist it, making the purl stitch tighter and therefore more distinct.

The origin of patterns for this type of textured knitting was probably woven damask fabrics, although many were also related to embroidery designs. Knitting, being a late-comer among textile construction techniques, has always been notorious for copying designs from other textile sources. Old folk knitters tended to lift design ideas from just about any surface embellishment, just as knitters do today.

Damask or brocade designs require a simple system of charting: dots to designate purl stitches on a plain ground.

Traveling Stitches and Cables

Textured designs featuring embossed or sculptured surfaces such as traveling stitches, cables, bobbles, trellises and honeycomb, require moving stitches or groups of stitches across the surface to realign their order. These three-dimensional designs were apparently were developed in Spain in the latter half of the 18th century, reaching their height in the Aran knitting of the late 19th and early 20th centuries.

Traveling stitches. Traveling stitches provide surface texture by moving diagonally left or right from row to row. These stitches actually lie on top of the fabric, in sharp relief to the background. If the stitch is twisted by working through the back loop, the raised effect is greater. Traveling stitches are usually worked in knit stitches on a purl ground. This type of work was often used to highlight and border the brocade patterns of the Danish blouse, and later reached the height of distinction in the Bavarian waistcoats popular in the alpine regions of Austria and Germany.

In its simplest form, the traveling stitch involves crossing two stitches, and doesn't require a cable needle. To work a left cross, that is a stitch leaning to the left on the surface, go *behind* the first stitch and work the second stitch; then work the first stitch, and slip both completed stitches off *together*. To work a right cross, go in *front* of the first stitch, work the second stitch, then the first stitch, slipping both stitches off *together*. The work is charted with a slash from one row diagonally to the next, showing the direction the stitch is traveling row to row. The diagonal line shows the new position of the stitch in the working row relative to its position in the former row. A word of caution when working twisted traveling stitches back and forth in flat knitting: both the knit stitch on the right side and the purl stitch on the reverse side must be twisted.

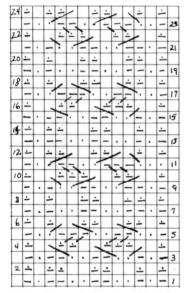

Traveling stitches graphed for flat knitting.

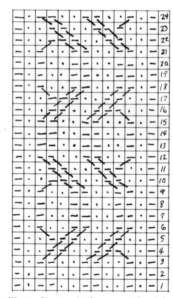

Traveling stitches graphed for circular knitting.

Cables. The simple cable was probably the earliest embossed work, and also the most widely adapted among many cultures. The cable is an extension of the traveling stitch; instead of a single stitch crossing the surface, a group of stitches is carried. Doing this move requires an auxiliary needle, such as a cable needle; a group of stitches is removed from the left needle to the cable needle without being worked, a group of stitches beyond these is worked, then the stitches on the cable needle are moved back into position on the left needle, or worked directly off the cable needle, to complete the sequence. To work a cable leaning left, place the stitches on the cable needle and hold them in *front* of the work. To work a cable leaning right, hold the stitches on the cable needle *behind* the work.

To chart cable patterns, use diagonal lines within the working row, one on each side of the group being realigned; the direction of the diagonals corresponds with the direction the stitches are to lean.

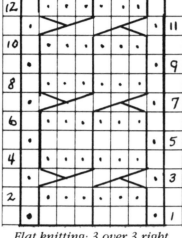

Flat knitting: 3 over 3 right cable

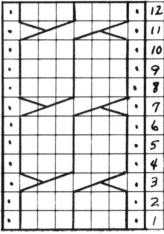

Circular knitting: 3 over 3 right cable

Trellis, honeycomb, and intricate braided designs are more elaborate than the simple cable, but the basic working technique is still only a matter of removing a series of stitches to an auxiliary needle so they can be worked in a different order than they were originally.

An elaboration of the cabling technique is the divided cable, in which the two sections are divided by one or more stitches. To accomplish this, you cable within the cable. The cable movement removes a series of stitches to reverse their order, with the left cable stitches removed to the front and the right cable stitches removed to the back. In the divided cable, the working order of the stitches on the cable needle is also reversed, front or back, depending on the direction of the lean required. This particular move can be charted in one of two ways, with the one method illustrating the working movements more clearly while the second method gives a clearer representation of the pattern. The twisted cable example shown here presents both methods, as well as written instructions.

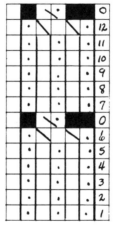

A divided cable showing use of two rows to complete a move.

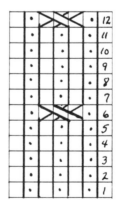

A divided cable showing move on one row.

Increase and Decrease Stitches. There are countless ways to increase and decrease to create a seemingly infinite number of pattern stitch variations. The increase-decrease can be used to alter the outline of design units, or it can be used to create sculptured units such as the bobble. It's difficult to generalize about this type of pattern element, although directional lean of the increase and decrease always corresponds to the direction of the outline of a design feature. Furthermore, the number of stitches within the individual rows should remain constant, with the number of increases equalling the number of decreases. Some lace stitch variations are exceptions. Charting these designs on graph paper requires flexibility in the use of the basic symbols.

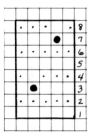

All over bobble in flat knitting.

For example, the bobble is worked within one row, but requires several little rows within that row to develop. To make a bobble, an initial stitch is increased, the work is turned and those two stitches worked, and turned and worked again. Several rows may be incorporated into a single bobble in this way. Therefore on the graph, the bobble would appear as a ' ● ', with a separate section, rather like a footnote, showing how to work the bobble.

A final note on charting intricate embossed patterns: it's hardly possible to chart these designs without having to use an asterisk to refer to additional instructions. But the primary purpose of charting is to clearly define the position of each design segment relative to the whole garment and to other pattern elements within the garment. The chart represents continuous rows across the pattern or patterns, so that it's easy to see at a glance what comes next. To further simplify a chart for, say, an Aran sweater, draw vertical lines between pattern sections in a contrasting color. Put split ring markers on your work to correspond to these lines, and you'll find it much easier to maintain order while your work is in progress.

All over bobble in circular knitting.

Also, as the number of rows required to complete an entire repeat will vary from pattern to pattern, a line drawn across the chart to denote the completion of the repeat is helpful. If the patterns have different numbers of rows, use a series of magnetic row markers, one for each pattern element if necessary, to maintain position.

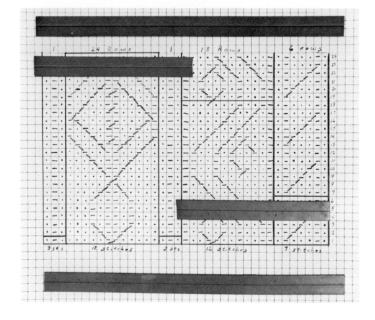

Charted design with magnetic strips placed above the row in progress. As the two sections have two different repeats, the strips are placed at different locations on each.

Two-Strand Textured Designs

Two-strand texture knitting is a traditional Scandinavian technique which fell into disuse in the 19th century. It's most often worked from both ends of the same ball, although it can be worked in two colors instead. Many old stockings and mittens which appear at first glance to be worked in stockinette stitch are actually worked with two strands of the same yarn alternating, doubling the fabric.

Traditionally, two-strand knitting was worked with both working strands in the right hand, with each stitch being knitted from beneath the strand of the previous stitch. This way of working, with the two yarns twisting around each other, makes a firm, double-thick fabric, but requires stopping to untwist the working strands frequently. A simpler way, which eliminates the twisting, is to work as for color stranding, with one yarn in each hand. This modified technique also doubles the thickness, but is more elastic and allows for decorative surface stitches.

The cast-on must be adapted to accommodate the additional strand. An easy way to do this is to tie the two strands together as illustrated, using two colors for easier learning. Use the long tails to form a twisted loop cast-on. Work the first loop with either of the two strands connected to the ball, snugging this loop into the knot. The second loop is formed with the second strand, coming from *under* the first strand to twist the two together. Work across in *alternate* strands, coming from *under* each time to twist the two together.

Casting on in two colors.

To knit in the traditional way, work each stitch alternately, twisting the yarns by going *under* the strand just used. The purl stitch is worked in the same way, working the stitches in alternate strands, and always bringing the yarn *under* the former strand. On the outside, the fabric looks just like regular stockinette, but the inside shows a surface of twisted strands.

In the simplified form, carry the two strands, one in each hand, and work alternately. This eliminates the twisting and tangling of the two balls, and it's faster, too.

You can create textured patterns in this technique with the chain stitch. To work it, bring a strand forward to the knit side, purl it, and carry the yarn across the surface while knitting a stitch with the other strand, then purl and return the first strand to the back. A regular repetition of chains across the row creates a decorative pattern.

Two strand chart.

Another decorative effect is done with purl knots made by purling a stitch with both strands at once. Charting this work on graph paper involves adding a chain symbol; if you want to denote purl knots worked with two strands, double the purl symbol.

Another texture can be made if you're working in two colors. Purl a row alternating colors, carrying the colors in front of the work instead of in back. Twist the two colors together as you go. On the next row, purl again with the strands in front, twisting them in the opposite direction. The effect will be a raised braid with a zig-zag pattern.

A swatch of textured two-strand knitting.

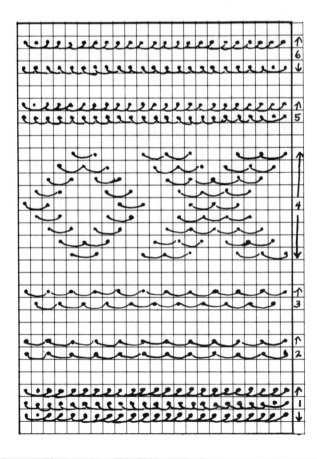

Chart for two-strand knitting swatch.

An effective way to keep cast-on/bound-off edges from rolling is to make several rows of twisted two-strand knitting worked in the traditional way with the twist between stitches. You can create a decorative edge by using two colors and carrying them on the front of the work, alternating the directions in which they twist as described above.

If you need to shape two-strand work, increase by knitting both yarns into one stitch, and then work each loop separately in the next round. Decreases are worked as usual.

Textured Sweaters of Denmark

The Danish brocade blouse, called *natrøje* or 'nightshirt', is the oldest sweater-like garment thought to have been worn by common folk. There is some question as to when it became part of the peasant costume, as the pieces that have survived in museums were from the upper classes. We surmise this because most are made of fine worsted yarn, or even of silk-wool blends—not what you'd expect to find among the working classes. They are copies of silk knit garments common among the royalty of that time, and would have entered the everyday wear of the upper classes before filtering down. We do know that the brocade blouse was incorporated early into the Danish women's costume, and offers splendid inspiration for knitters today.

The brocade blouse varied from a short garment with short sleeves to a long blouse with long sleeves. It was worked from the lower edge with the front and back separate, most often in a diced knit-purl welt. After several rows the two parts were joined at the underarm seamlines and worked in the round to the armhole, which included a small half-gusset. The work was then divided front and back and worked to the shoulder with a square neck opening which was bound with fabric later. On early pieces, the front neck often included an applique'd overlay of woven brocade fabric. The over-all design was usually copied from woven damask fabrics, and occasionally included twisted traveling stitches in an interesting ribbon-fold design. The side seamlines were two purl stitches emphasized on either side with decorative bands in knit-purl patterns or twisted traveling stitches. These decorative bands were carried all the way to the shoulder strap, which was then worked as a flap and bound off together on the inside.

An interesting parallel in both construction and patterning exists between these blouses, worn exclusively by women, and the gansey of Great Britain, worn exclusively by men. Both feature a split welt, side seamline, gusset, and similar working technique. Where, do you suppose, did this garment truly originate?

Another puzzle: On Amager Island, off the coast of Denmark, lived a wealthy group of Dutch descent who, at one period, wore a traditional bodice of indigo blue or black woven fabric with knitted sleeves worked in complex knit-purl patterns, apparently copied from the clock patterns of stockings. The Amager women excelled in fine embroidery, and portions of

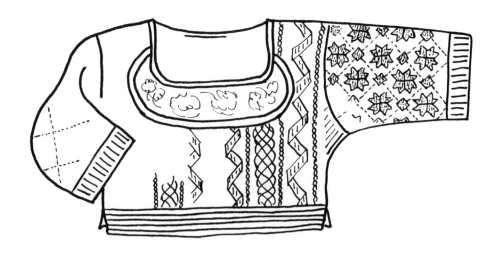

Danish Brocade Blouse, short version

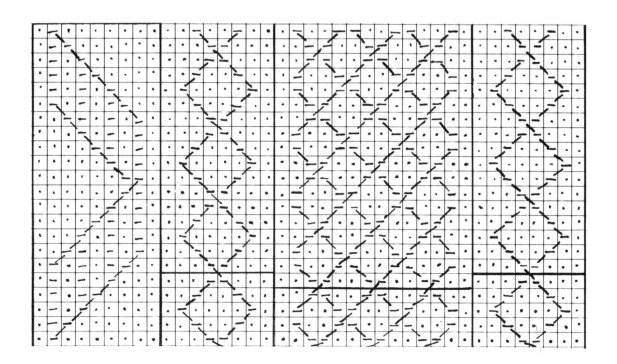

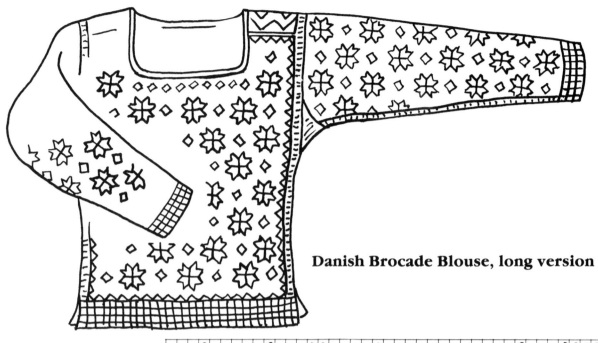

Danish Brocade Blouse, long version

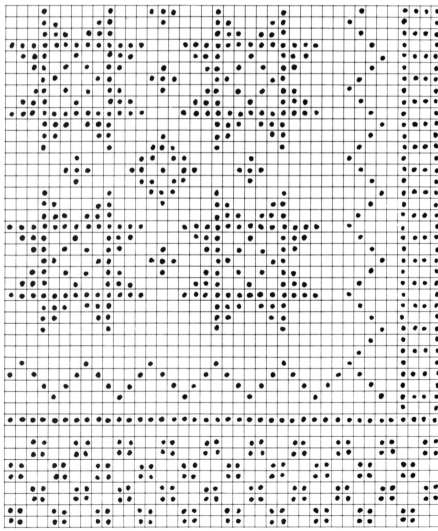

Stitches for Danish Brocade Blouse, beginning with diced welt

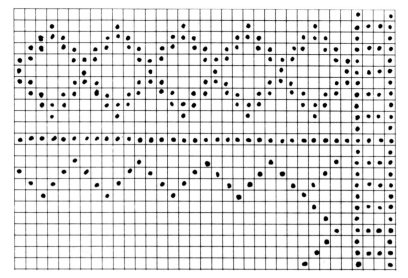

Pattern across shoulders.

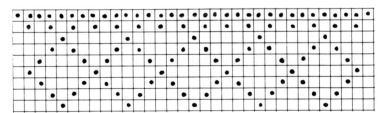

Pattern at lower front neck edge.

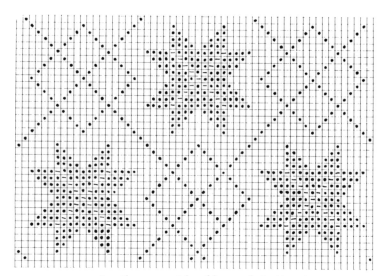

Another example of brocade patterning.

the designs—peacocks, crowns, stars, flowers—might have come from embroidery sources. Though this garment was part of the regular costume of this group, the women themselves did not knit. Knitting wasn't considered suitable for women of their station, so they had the knitting done by their Swedish maids. A similar cloth-bodice jacket with knitted sleeves, color stranded instead of textured, was part of the Swedish national costume. Where did the garment originate—with the Dutch Amager, or the Swedish maids? It's an intriguing question.

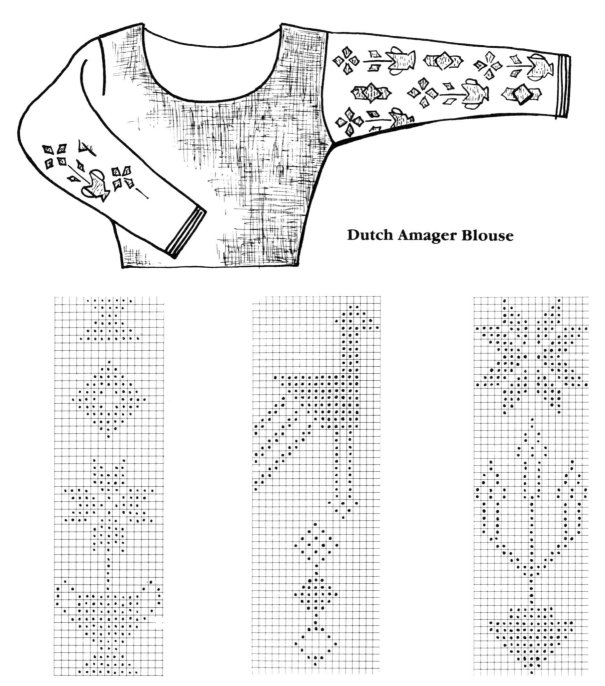

Dutch Amager Blouse

Pattern motifs used in Dutch Amager blouse.

Textured Knitting of Great Britain

In Great Britain, 'gansey' refers to a seaman's jersey. The term apparently originated on the Channel Islands of Guernsey and Jersey; both islands' names describe a pullover sweater, with gansey a slang term to describe pullovers in general. A standard construction technique was followed in making these seamless garments. The cast-on was done with a double yarn for durability. They were knit in the round to the underarm, with a gusset added for ease, and the work was divided front and back at the armholes. A shoulder strap provided depth for the neck opening. The sleeves were picked up and worked just short of the wrist, with the edge bound off in doubled yarn. Simple knit-purl patterns were worked on the upper chest, in time becoming more elaborate with the addition of cables and the extension of the patterned area to the upper arms and then to the entire body and sleeves. In early times, patterns could be used to identify people of a particular village, but over the years they spread by being copied until they lost their regionality.

The earliest ganseys were not necessarily made of the fine five-ply navy worsted (often called "seaman's iron") identified with them today. More often they were a coarser two-ply woolen. Multiple-ply fine knitting worsteds didn't come into common use until the advent of spinning mills. Worsted yarns were common in hosiery for the upper classes, and as the gansey was an outgrowth of hosiery knitting, use of a similar yarn was natural when it became available.

On the islands of the Hebrides, particularly Eriskey Isle, the gansey reached new heights of textured design. Early Hebridean ganseys were very similar to those of the rest of Great Britain, although the pattern elements were distributed differently. There is little doubt that a more ornate style developed during the 20th century; quite possibly, these newer designs were influenced by Aran patterns. The Aran influence began in the 1930s when Heinze E. Kiewe first brought Aran sweaters to public attention. He spent the next 30 years collecting and recording Aran patterns, which he had worked by contract knitters on the Hebrides. But regardless of their origin, these garments are distinctly Hebridean in character and a highly developed folk art. Even today, these fine ganseys are produced by hand for sale.

The Hebridean gansey has two separate sets of pattern motifs. The lower body has simple knit-purl patterned panels; it is divided from the yoke by a horizontal welt, often in a mesh pattern. The yoke is more complex, with vertical panels divided into square blocks of different patterns and the panels themselves sometimes divided by cables. It is in the square blocks that today's ganseys have become more elaborate, often including openwork. The shoulder straps are worked as flaps at the top of the sweater front, and are bound off together with the back to close the shoulder. A mesh design is often used on the straps. The collar is picked up and knit back and forth, and includes an underlap to allow for buttoning. The sleeves of older styles were often plain stockinette stitch, but today they often repeat the pattern of the lower body.

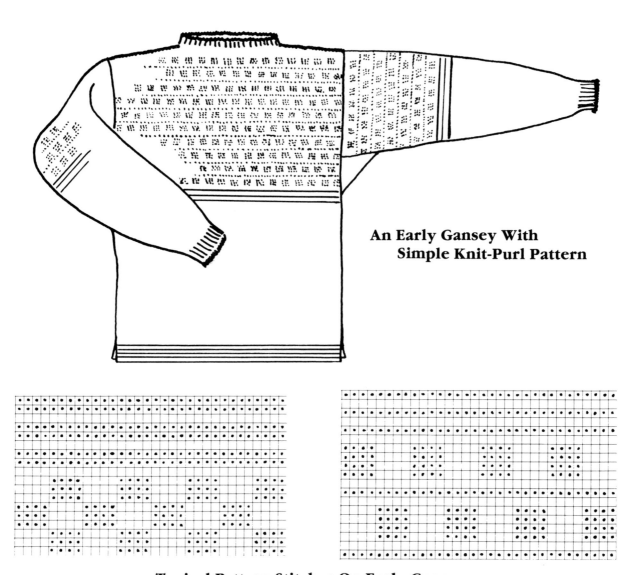

**An Early Gansey With
Simple Knit-Purl Pattern**

Typical Pattern Stitches On Early Ganseys

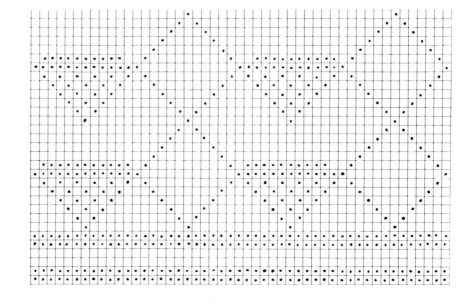

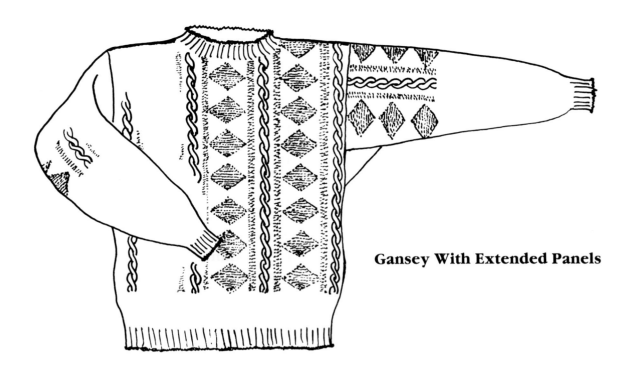

Gansey With Extended Panels

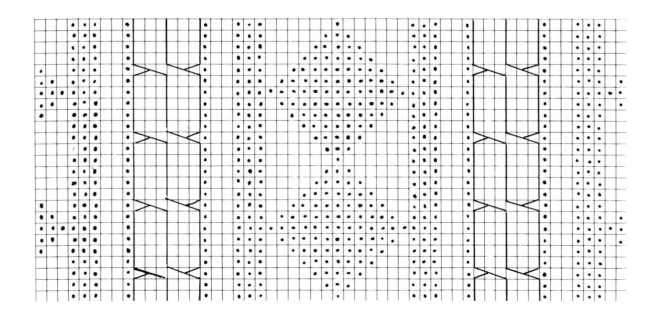

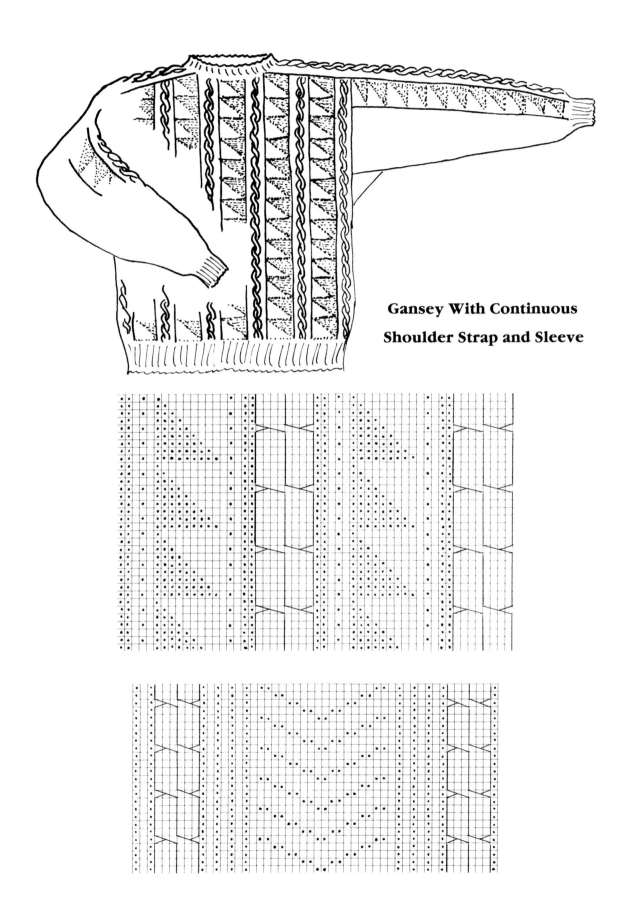

**Gansey With Continuous
Shoulder Strap and Sleeve**

The Gansey

Since mill-spun yarns became readily available in the mid-1800s, the standard yarn for the fisherman's gansey has been a fine five-ply worsted. Earlier, this sweater type was made of handspun, usually a heavier two-ply. I knit this example in a two-ply worsted of the traditional navy blue. It measured 14 wraps per inch, and has about 8 twists per inch. I used size 6 needles for a gauge of 5½ stitches per inch. I wanted a yarn that would work up fairly quickly and yet be fine enough to give me plenty of stitches to develop the patterns.

I used Plan 2, with a shaped crew neck. I used a double strand of yarn for cast on and bound off edges, which gives a cabled effect often found on traditional ganseys. Instead of the old split welt, though, I worked a K2, P2 ribbing. There's a P2 side seam on either side extending up from one of the P2 ribs.

The sweater is worked entirely in knit-purl patterns and symmetrically placed simple cables. Instead of shoulder straps, I continued the pattern all the way to the shoulder line and bound front and back off together on the outside for a decorative finish. Thus the entire garment is seamless, just as ganseys of old.

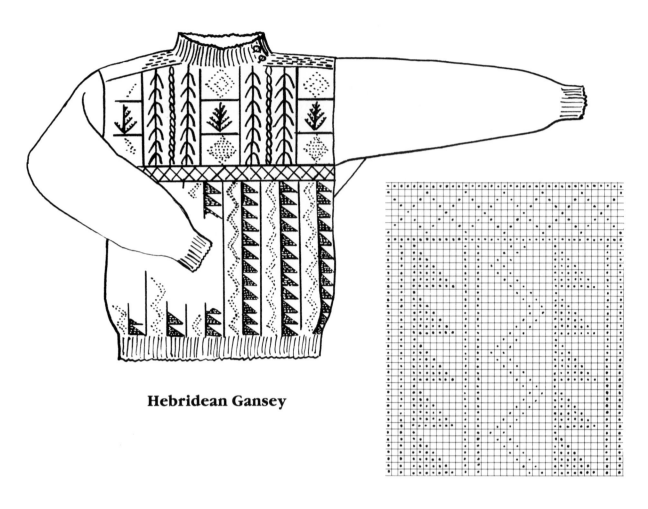

Hebridean Gansey

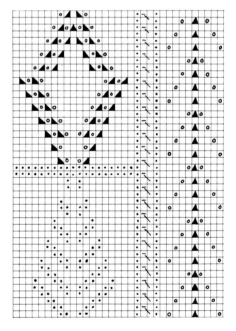

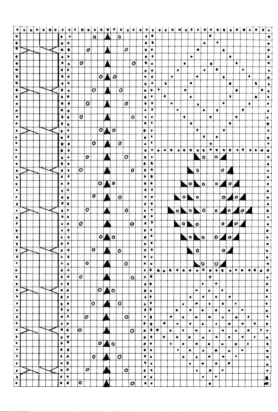

Textured Sweaters of the Netherlands

Coastal villagers of the Netherlands depended on the sea for their livelihood. These fishermen began to wear sweaters by the mid-19th century, both handknits of local origin and frame-knitted garments imported from England and Belgium. The knitters of these villages apparently adapted the designs of Great Britain, their neighbors to the west, while the basic shaping was similar to that used in Scandinavia to the north. But in the hands of local knitters, the Dutch fisherman's sweater developed a distinctive style, some elements of which were associated with certain geographical areas. The common practice was for each fisherman to have two sweaters, one heavily felted of thick yarns for wear on the sea, and one of finer yarns, often elaborately patterned, for wear on shore.

They were knit of a common and inexpensive domestic wool yarn called *sajet* (pronounced sah-yet', and meaning "firm twist" in Dutch). As local sheep were raised primarily for meat, their wool was short and coarse, requiring the firm twist for which it was named. The yarn was dyed in several colors, including blue, beige, gray, and black; the most popular was called Nassau blue after the Dutch royal family. This particular color was dark blue with red fibers spun in which gave the knitwear a reddish heather tone. *Sajet* became less popular after World War II when knitters no longer had to be so thrifty and many began to choose synthetics.

The seamless fisherman's sweater was knit in the round, beginning with a K2, P2 ribbing. The boxy shape of the garment was based on division by thirds. The total length was divided by three, two-thirds of the length to the underarm and one-third for the armhole. As the patterns were mostly knit-purl with simple cables that could be worked flat easily, the work was divided into front and back at the armhole and worked flat to the shoulder. Three to five platform stitches allow for ease at the underarm. The width was divided into thirds, one for each shoulder and one for the neck. The front neck stitches were removed about 2″ below the top of the shoulder, but the neck opening wasn't shaped. The shoulders were bound off together, and the sleeve picked up at the armhole and worked down to the wrist. The neckband was worked in ribbing, often with eyelets for a drawstring to make it snug. The drawstring was often decorated with pom-pons on the ends.

Many Dutch fisherman sweaters resembled the British gansey, with textured patterns across the upper body and all-over cabled patterns. Others were patterned sampler-fashion, and some had only a single motif at center front, usually a God's eye or anchor. Early sweaters of this latter style were first machine knit, and later copied by local knitters.

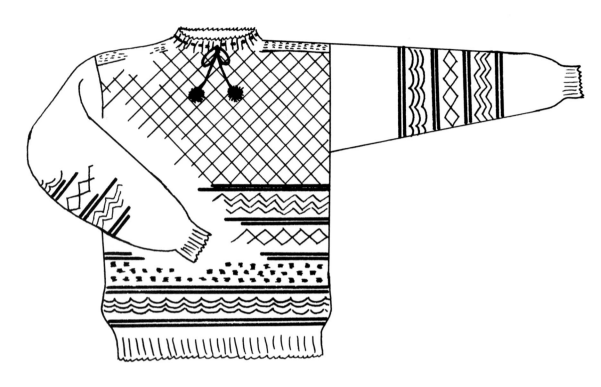

Sampler Style Dutch Fisherman Sweater

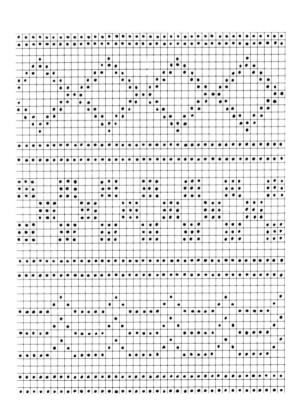

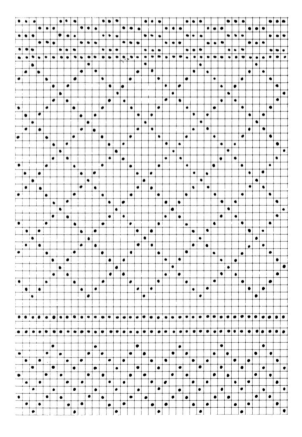

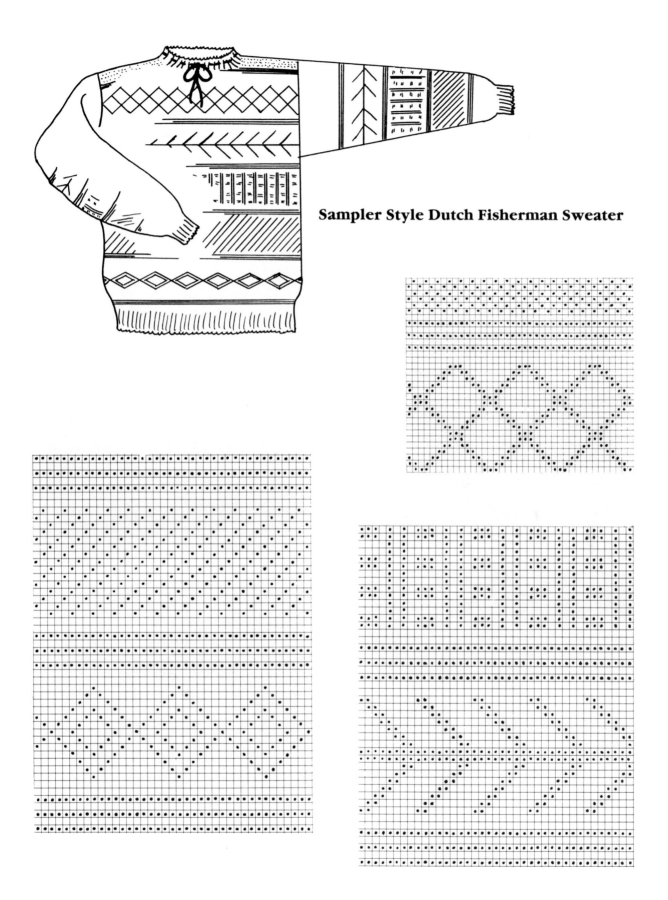

Sampler Style Dutch Fisherman Sweater

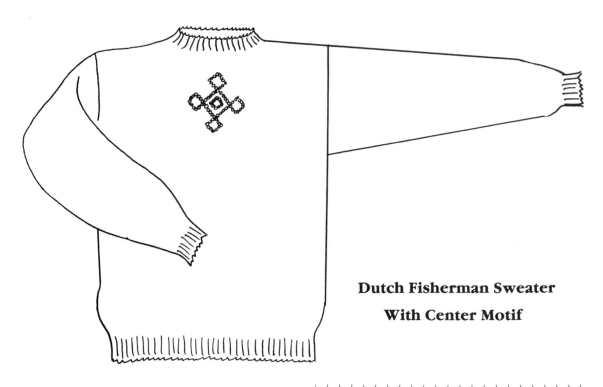

Dutch Fisherman Sweater
With Center Motif

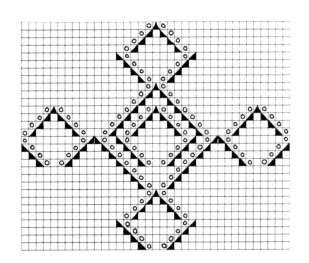

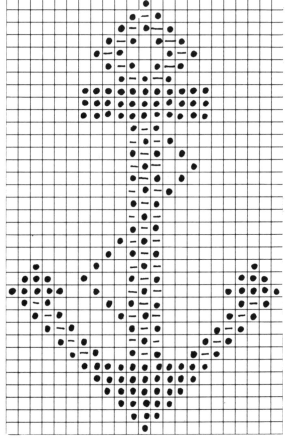

Textured Sweaters of Ireland

Off the coast of Ireland lie three islands, the Arans, home of the Aran fishing shirt. No other type of knitted garment has had more mythical qualities attributed to it, nor more controversy surrounding it. Although many early knitted garments are documented through letters and cottage industry inventories, not so with the Aran. Its history is largely unknown.

What we do know is that the Aran fishing shirt was first brought to public attention in 1936. Heinze Kiewe recorded and photographed this remarkable garment, and then proceeded to devote 30 years to collecting patterns which, as mentioned earlier, he had knitted for him on the Hebridean Islands. In studying old documents and Celtic art, particularly the Book of Kells, Kiewe developed a theory that dated the Aran sweater in antiquity, and he gave names attributing early Christian religious significance to various patterns.

It's easier, though, to justify a more recent origin for the Aran sweater; to argue, in fact, that it's probably a product of the 20th century. In the first place, there are no written records of its earlier existence. Second, they are knitted of natural white yarn—an impractical color that was astutely avoided by most early folk knitters. Furthermore, there were knitters in the 1940s who clearly recalled that it was the typical British gansey style that was traditionally knit on the islands, not the fishing shirt with its heavily embossed patterns. But the old knitters of Aran are now dead or dispersed, so the mystery of how and when they originated continues. Fortunately, Gladys Thompson recorded these garments, and her research is published for posterity.

Whether ancient or modern, the garments are distinctive, with bobbles, cables and interlacing stitches providing deep surface relief. There is further controversy about how they were constructed: were they always knit in sections and sewn together (as they often are today), or were they originally worked in the round the old way? Museum specimens in Dublin were made by contract workers, not by the Aran islanders themselves, so they could easily have been worked according to current techniques. Thompson has stated that they were most likely knitted in the round, and most authorities on traditional knitting agree with her. Early examples were more than likely made in the classic circular way, with the shift to flat pieces coming as the designs became more complex. Although based on similar techniques, many of the complex modern designs have evolved a long way from the early Aran designs.

All arguments aside, the garments themselves are lovely. They are knit of a thick, creamy woolen yarn called *bainin* (pronounced 'bawneen' and meaning 'natural'), and they feature deeply embossed patterns. The early fishing shirts consisted of a deep 'skirt' of small cables instead of a ribbed welt. It was separated from the main body with a ridge of purling or garter stitch. The body of the garment included a center panel equal in width to the front neck, flanked on each side by vertical pattern panels. The sleeves were knit with deep cuffs of ribbing which sometimes included small cables, and worked with a center panel that extended to the neck, forming a shoulder strap. The sleeve panels generally repeated some portion of the

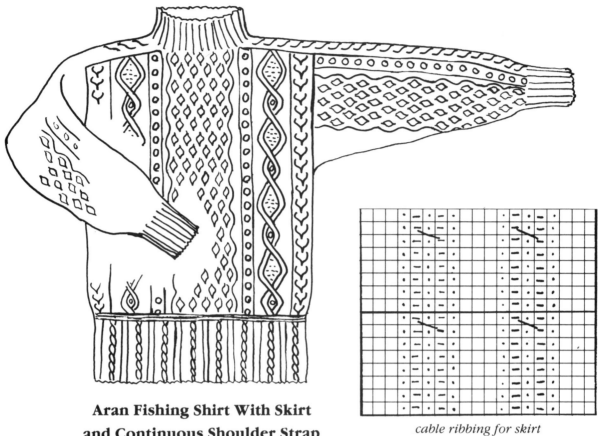

**Aran Fishing Shirt With Skirt
and Continuous Shoulder Strap**

cable ribbing for skirt

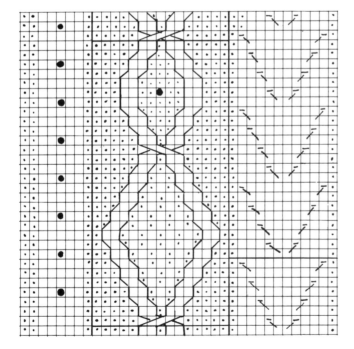

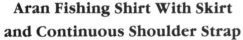

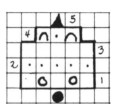

bobble chart

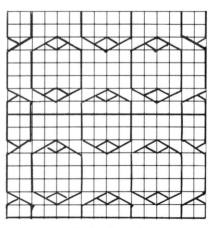

center panel

Aran Fishing Shirt

This sweater is knit of a bulky three-ply worsted measuring 7 wraps per inch, and knitted at a gauge of 3½ stitches per inch on number 10 needles. I designed it for rugged outdoor wear, and the yarn is right for that purpose. But because of its bulk, there weren't enough stitches to allow for as many embossed panels as you'd find in a traditional sweater. As is often the case, it was a matter of balancing one feature against another.

I followed Plan 9—a traditional boxy shape with a 'skirt' which includes cables, a saddle shoulder strap, deep cuff and neckband. I worked this one flat instead of round—seems as though we must remind ourselves now and then just what an irksome project sewing unnecessary seams can be!

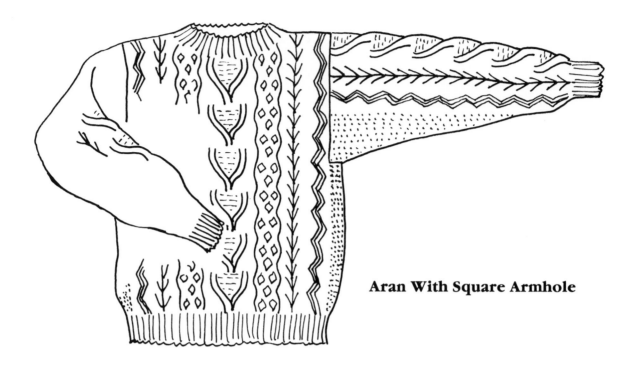

Aran With Square Armhole

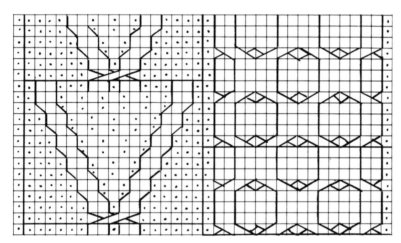

center section

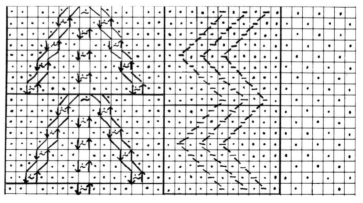

side section

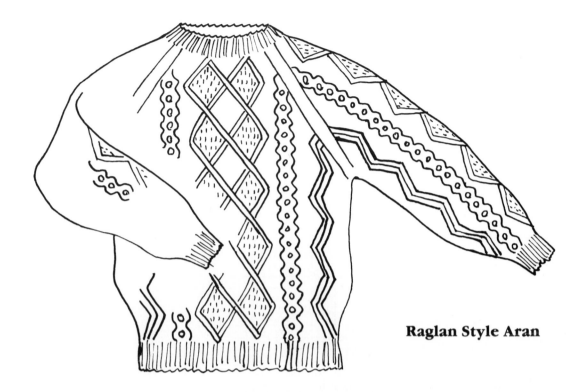

Raglan Style Aran

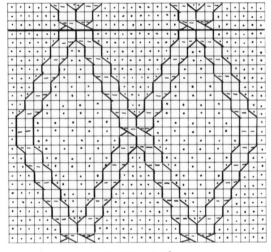

center panel

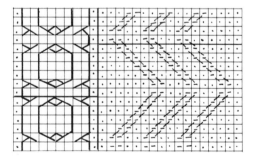

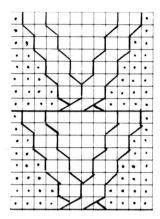

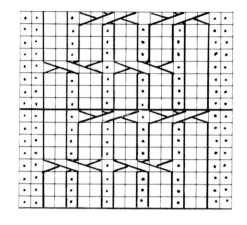

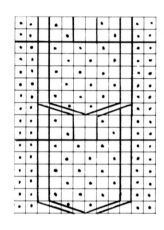

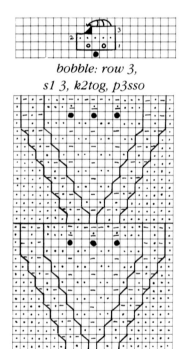

bobble: row 3,
s1 3, k2tog, p3sso

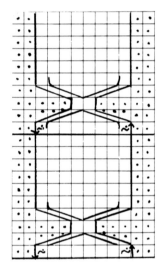

Additional Popular Aran Panels

body pattern, but not necessarily in the same order or the same width. The neck band was a deep ribbing reaching to the chin, sometimes with cables.

Later examples often omitted the shoulder strap, and continued the body pattern across the shoulders instead. The shoulder line was sloped for a closer fit, and the cabled skirt was also omitted.

Today's Arans are usually raglan style. The commercially produced ones lack spontaneity in the patterning, with many being worked in bulky yarns which limit the number of stitches and thus the pattern complexity.

Textured Sweaters of Norway

In the Dalarna region of Norway, the old technique of two strand knitting often found in thick woolen mittens and stocking tops has recently been rediscovered. In the 19th century, this technique was applied to jackets. They were knit from two strands of yarn, both of the same color (mitten bands were often worked in two colors). The yarns twisted between stitches, resulting in a very firm, non-elastic garment of double thickness. These jackets have bands of textured patterns created by bringing one strand forward, purling it, allowing it to travel across the surface of a stitch, purling it again, then returning it to the back. This technique is described on page 128; you can see it in the second band from the top on the cover of this book. Early garments using this patterning technique were more than likely worked in the round, cut, and then bound with fabric.

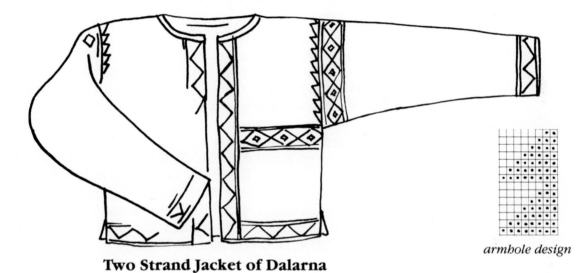

Two Strand Jacket of Dalarna

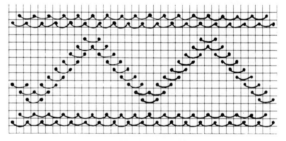

armhole design

begin at edges

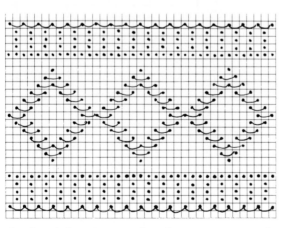

horizontal center panel and upper arm panel

153

Textured Sweaters of Austria and Germany

The alpine regions of Austria and Germany have beautiful traditional styles that have much in common with the work of the Aran Islands. Where did these designs come from? Did the Aran, Bavarian, and Tyrolean styles spring from the same source? At this time these questions can't be answered, but the beauty of the work is undisputed.

The Bavarian designs are richly textured and embossed with twisted traveling stitches, a style of patterning first worked in elegant stockings. As in other cultures, the designs migrated from hosiery to other garments, in this case to waistcoats and jackets. Little information about the earliest of these garments is available, but we can assume that they were usually snug fitting. Remember, this is the land of the dirndl skirt, and a jersey-style sweater would not be in keeping with the national costume. Furthermore, cutting and felting knitted fabric was a common practice in this region; some of the early tailored 'boiled wool' jackets might well have been made of felted and brushed knitted fabrics, as they are today.

Bavarian knitted jackets are snugly shaped waist-length cardigans with scooped necks and richly patterned panels. Typically, panels of traveling stitch motifs were worked down each side of the center front opening and repeated down the center back; the rest was worked in simple all-over knit-purl patterns. The men's jackets were usually slightly longer and less elaborate than the women's, and often omitted the center back panel.

There is little known, either, about early Tyrolean sweaters, but by the early 20th century garments relied on the use of cables and bobbles rather than on twisted traveling stitches. In this way they bear more resemblance to the work of Aran knitters. A unique feature of these garments, though, is bits of embroidery—small flashes of color such as you would expect to find in alpine meadows when the wildflowers bloom. The embroidery embellishes and emphasizes the structural design. Like the Bavarian jacket, the Tyrolean is snug fitting and waist length, to wear with a dirndl skirt.

The Berchtesgaden sweater is a simple style which relies on color contrast for design interest. The body is knit in black, and trimmed in vivid red and green. The snug fit is accentuated with a drawstring tie at the waist and often at the scoop neck as well. Early examples were probably felted and cut to shape, with the red and green accents covering the cut edges. Today this sweater is knit in a ribbing stitch throughout. The scoop neck is finished with an insert of the contrast colors; its stitches are picked up and worked much like a collar, with a drawstring to pull it together for a close fit.

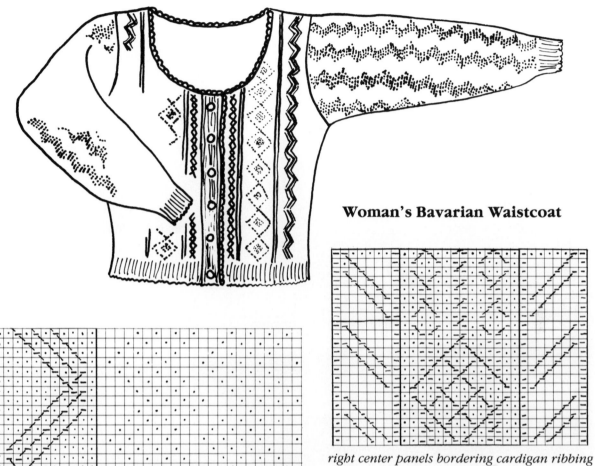

Woman's Bavarian Waistcoat

right center panels bordering cardigan ribbing

sleeve design

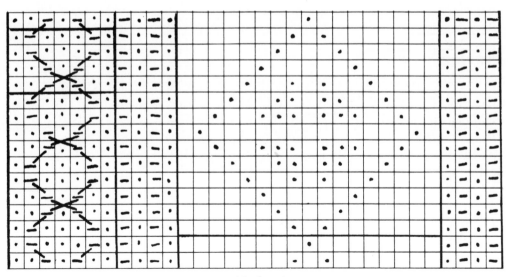

side front

Detail showing right side of vest back.

Bavarian Vest

There's a pleasant rhythm to working this sweater's textured pattern in the round. It's created entirely of single twisted traveling stitches. The yarn, a firmly spun two-ply true worsted (13 wraps per inch and 8 twists per inch), gives the pattern clear definition. My gauge was 5½ stitches per inch. The only thing that gave me problems knitting this piece was the color—in less than perfect light, the pattern got lost.

I used Formulas 14 and 16, using a steek so I could continue working in the round. The buttonhole overlap is knitted, but the underlap is grosgrain ribbon. With so many buttons, I thought the ribbon would stabilize the front and hold its shape better. I picked up stitches and knit ribbing around the neck and armholes. There were a lot of cut edges to work down, but this seemed preferable to trying to knit the traveling stitch pattern flat.

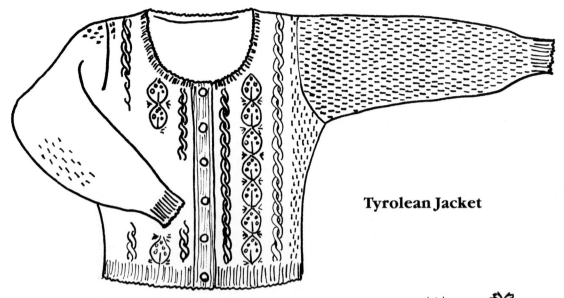

Tyrolean Jacket

embroidery design

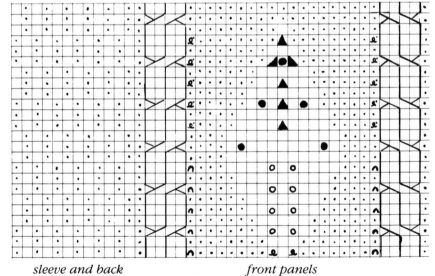

sleeve and back   *front panels*

●bobble: row 1, purl in front and back loop twice
          row 2, k4
          row 3, p4
          row 4, slip stitches 2,3 and 4 over first st,
          then slip to right needle.

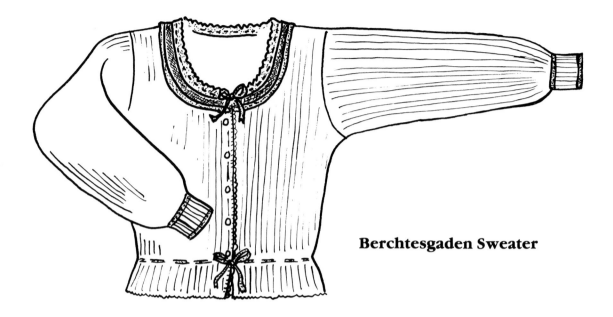

Berchtesgaden Sweater

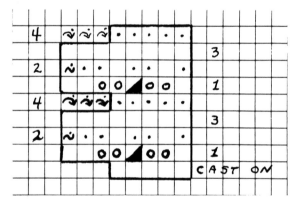

lace neck edging

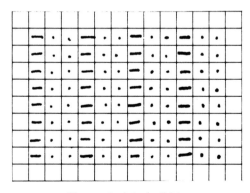

all-over twisted ribbing

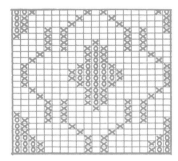

Sweaters with Geometric Pattern

Geometric patterns in knitting can be achieved through color contrast or directional knitting. Both have been used in interesting folk sweaters.

The Striped Farmhand's Sweater of Denmark

Narrow horizontal stripes of blue and white were fairly common in undershirts of the early 19th century, especially among Danish farmhands. This garment was usually knit in the round to the armhole, divided and worked to the neck with shoulder straps grafted, a narrow neckband applied, and sleeves worked from shoulder to wrist. They were functional garments, snug in body and sleeve, and usually worn under a vest of some sort during working hours.

Here's a simple way to avoid the staggered join where the rounds meet. Knit the first stitch of each new stripe with *both* colors. Continue knitting around, completing the first row of the new stripe and the joining double stitch. Then carefully pull the strand of yarn from the previous stripe to hide it beneath the new color.

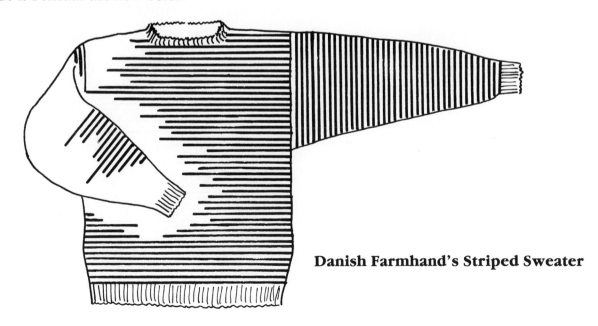

Danish Farmhand's Striped Sweater

Basketweave Sweaters of Finland

Across the Scandinavian and Nordic countries, a geometric type of knitting which resembles woven basketry was popular for caps and mittens, and occasionally used in waistcoats, too. This type of work was particularly striking in Finland, where it was worked in dramatically contrasting red and black. Basketweave is easily worked into sweaters, and is particularly effective in the yoke; an entire sweater might be a little overwhelming unless worked in one color only.

Basketweave can be worked round or flat. To set up the work, construct a base row of triangles above the ribbing or welt. The total stitches must be an even number, divisible by the number of stitches in the basketweave unit. The stitches in each unit must also be an even number; I will use six as an example. The number of rows in each unit is twice the number of stitches, i.e., 12 in the example. Make the base row of triangles as follows:

K2, turn; P2, turn; K3, turn; P3, turn; K4, turn; P4, turn; K5, turn; P5, turn; K6.

Repeat this sequence for each triangle across the row. To work in the round, begin the first row of squares:

Pick up 6 stitches along the side of the first triangle, and turn. K6, turn; P5, P2tog (last picked up stitch and first triangle stitch), turn; K5, turn; P4, P2tog, turn; continue to work in this way until all the stitches of the triangle have been worked off.

Repeat around until the first row of squares is complete. Work the second row of squares as before, except that the knit and purl rows will be reversed, and the last two stitches will be worked together as a SSK decrease. Continue in this manner until you've reached the desired depth, working the final row as triangles. To work the final triangles, leave one stitch unworked at the edge of every second row, reducing the stitches by half—back to the original number on the needles before you began the basketweave section. Bind off the edge, or resume working stockinette stitch.

If you're working flat, work each side in triangles, not squares. Do this by decreasing the outside edge by one stitch at the end of every second row.

Direction of work for basketweave knitting.

160

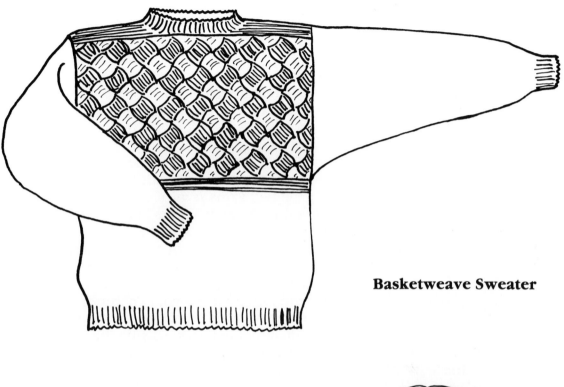

Basketweave Sweater

The Argyle Sweater of Scotland

The argyle sweater was adapted from stockings, as were many other sweater styles. Early leggings were of woven fabric—tartan, in Scotland. Flexibility was gained by using the fabric on the bias, and argyle knitting produces a pattern similar in appearance to bias tartan. Argyle patterns are worked flat, and usually only the sweater front is patterned. The argyle sweater is a product of the 20th century. It is shaped at the armhole, and usually has a V neck.

This is *not* a color stranding technique, but rather a bobbin technique. When a design such as the argyle requires blocks or sections of color rather than small groups of stitches, each section is worked from a separate bobbin or ball of yarn to avoid carrying the yarn along the back of the fabric. The yarn for each color section is carried on its own bobbin. When a section is completed, its bobbin is left behind an a new one picked up. To avoid holes in the work, always pick up the new color from *beneath* the completed color, interlocking the two yarns at the changing point. To keep the bobbins from tangling as you work, punch holes in the side of a shoe box, one for each color, and run the yarns through them.

A true argyle pattern has an overlying pattern of diagonal lines. The yarns for the diagonals don't stay in sequence because they must travel left and right across the diamonds. Their bobbins shouldn't be put in the shoe box, but rather allowed to hang free to move left or right as necessary. Since a pair of diagonals starts from one point, wind a small bobbin at *each* end of a length of yarn. Begin the first stitches of the diagonal with the center of the yarn length; this will allow the diagonal to move both right and left from the same initial point.

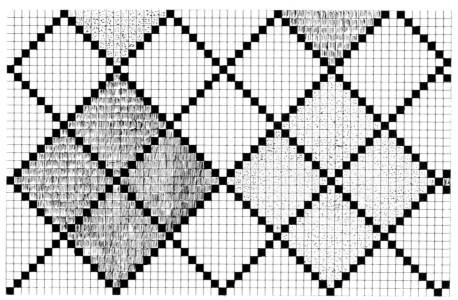

Argyle dicing in three colors with diagonals in a fourth color.

A modern application of bobbin techniques is the interpretation of patchwork quilts on sweater fronts. These same techniques can be used to knit pictorial designs from folk art sources such as early American samplers, Hispanic colcha embroideries, American Indian motifs, and others.

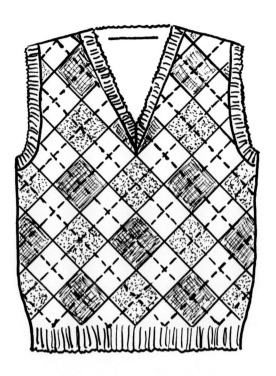

A Scottish Argyle Vest

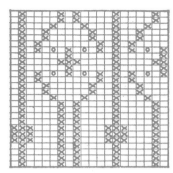

Spinning Techniques

While knitting is one of the youngest of the textile crafts, spinning is among the oldest. The spinning process consists of drawing out and twisting a group of fibers so they hold together in a strand, while regularly adding more fibers to extend its length. Thus a yarn is born. The process is fundamentally the same for mill produced yarns and handspun ones.

Because a knit fabric is constructed from a continuous strand of yarn in interlocking loops, the breaking of one weak loop will make a hole, eventually causing a section of the fabric to run. Thus spinning a consistently sound yarn is important to the durability of the fabric. Furthermore, the character of the yarn determines to a large extent the visual character and physical properties of the fabric made from it. It is essential to coordinate fiber and type of yarn with the knitted garment design. Whether you select a commercially spun yarn or handspin your own, some knowledge of spinning and yarn structure is very valuable.

I'd like to share with you my approach to spinning yarns that are appropriate for traditional sweater styles. If you don't already know the basics of spinning, consult one of the sources listed in the bibliography for basic instruction.

Fleece Selection

Selecting a fleece is often difficult, especially for the novice. Wool breed charts are available with various grading systems, including blood (the oldest system, based on the amount of Merino or Rambouillet in the breed), count (the number of 560 yard hanks that can be spun from one pound), and microns (actual fiber diameter as measured with a micrometer). Although breed is a good predictor of fiber fineness, these charts are often as confusing as they are helpful because characteristics of a breed aren't consistent from one flock to another, or even within the same flock. Age, sex and health of a sheep, plus diet and climate, can affect the quality of its fleece.

Other factors being equal, fineness is the first quality I look for in selecting fleece for knitting yarns. You don't need to be able to grade the fleece, but only to assess the degree of fiber fineness. It's helpful to know that fiber crimp is often directly related to fiber fineness; the finer the crimp, the finer the fiber. The fiber should be fine in proportion to the fineness of the yarn you intend to spin. If you plan to spin a yarn for fine lace knitting, look for a very fine fleece (such as Merino, Rambouillet or Cormo). For a sport weight yarn, choose a medium fine fiber such as Columbia, while a bulkier yarn calls for a medium fiber such as Romney or Corriedale. Refer to the chart on page 176 for a listing of some breeds and their suitability for knitting yarns.

Another important property to consider in selecting a fleece is "hand", a quality that's as difficult to define as it is to evaluate. Hand is the term used to describe how the wool feels—whether it's soft and pleasant, crisp and springy, or harsh and scratchy. You can best evaluate it by lightly scouring an individual lock with a short soak in a pan of warm sudsy water. Rinse it and blot it dry with an absorbent towel. If this clean sample feels good on your cheek, neck, or some equally delicate spot, you can assume it will feel good made into a garment—*if* it's appropriately spun.

There are other fiber properties that must be taken into account, too. A smooth, lustrous fiber will produce a silky yarn with good drape, whereas a springy, highly crimped fiber will yield a bouncy yarn. Crimp affects elasticity. A fiber with loose, wavy crimp is less elastic than one with tight, regular crimp. Also the more crimp in a fleece, the loftier a yarn you can spin from it. These qualities will be carried into your yarn and final fabric.

Consider fiber length, too, for it will determine to some degree whether you spin a woolen or worsted yarn. Generally speaking, fibers ranging from 1″ to 3″ are better spun as woolen yarns, fibers ranging from 3″-5″ can be spun with either method, while longer ones are more suitable for worsted spinning. The chart on page 176 includes some of the breeds available in the U.S. that are most suitable for knitting yarns. All have good hand and crimp combined with sufficiently fine fibers. The length designations are based on averages; considerable overlap may exist from fleece to fleece or within a given breed.

A fleece may vary considerably from one part of the body to another. Shoulder and side fleece is often finer than that on the flanks. You can sort a single fleece according to variations in fineness, fiber length, crimp, and hand, or you can simply "skirt" it, discarding the dirtiest parts from around the edges, and thoroughly blend all the remaining parts together so that your yarn will be uniform.

Always make your fleece selection with the end product in mind. Going out and purchasing a fleece just for the sake of having it, or because it's a good buy, doesn't make much sense when it comes time to spin. You need to select fleece with a yarn type and garment design in mind.

Fiber Preparation

Scouring. Once you've selected a suitable fleece, the key to making a quality knitting yarn is fiber preparation. You may choose to work "in the grease", with all the natural oils, etc., left in the fleece, or you can scour the wool to some degree. Long ago, fleece was probably spun in the grease more often than not, at least in those areas where water wasn't abundant. Often, the sheep were "washed" by being herded through a body of water before being sheared.

If you choose to spin in the grease, the fleece must be quite free of dirt and vegetable matter, and it must be freshly sheared. Storing it for even a short period of time makes the natural oils sticky. Teasing and carding will be difficult, and you'll find it hard to spin a consistent yarn.

Most spinners find that they can spin a finer, more uniform yarn working with a scoured fleece. It's not necessary to remove *all* the natural oils—only the stickiness and dirt, plus a lot of unpleasant aroma. The oils retained after a light scouring will oxidize and become sticky again in time, though, so you should process only as much as you can spin in a matter of days or perhaps weeks.

Woolen Preparation.   First, shake the fleece to remove loose material, then pick off large pieces of straw, burrs, and other debris. Put the fleece in a large mesh laundry bag, but don't pack it tightly; water must be able to circulate freely. Fill a tub that's large enough to accommodate the fleece loosely with comfortably hot water (100°-110° F.), and add enough mild, neutral detergent to make the water feel slick. Fleeces like Merino with high oil content require more detergent than less oily ones like Dorset. Incidentally, you don't have to use an expensive or hard-to-find detergent; most liquid dish detergents, such as Sunlight® , my favorite, are perfectly suitable.

Gently submerge the fleece and let it soak, turning the bag occasionally. Let it soak two to four hours (the stickier the fleece, the longer the soak), and then drain it, pressing the bag to remove excess water. Refill the tub with warm-to-the-hand water, but don't let the water run directly onto the fleece, as this can cause felting. Let the fleece soak in this rinse until the water is completely cool. Additional rinses may be necessary if the fleece was extremely dirty. Then drain and press out the excess water. You can put the mesh bag of fleece in your washing machine and run the spin cycle only; the centrifugal force won't damage your fleece, and it can greatly decrease the drying time.

Remove the fleece from the bag, and fluff and spread it to dry in a well-ventilated area away from the direct sun. A sweater rack or fiberglass window screen works well. Turn the fleece occasionally to speed drying.

A light scouring like this doesn't strip the fleece of all its natural oils, it only removes dirt and excess grease. More oil can be removed by repeated soakings with detergent. If you're afraid of over-scouring, remember that it's easier to apply a little spinning oil than to struggle with a sticky, greasy fleece.

If your fleece has been stored for a long time and become very sticky, you may want to do a more thorough scouring. The procedure I use is the same as above, but with more heat. Put the fleece in a large enamel or stainless steel pot and place it on the stove burner set at medium heat. Bring it to a slow simmer, about 150°-180°. After it comes to a simmer, remove it from the burner and let it cool, and then proceed as for a light scouring. Adding a little olive oil or baby oil—a tablespoon or two per gallon—to the final rinse water will make the fibers easier to handle and less subject to damage in the carding process.

When the wool is dry, tease the locks (open and fluff them by hand) to remove extraneous matter and second cuts. Or you can use a mechanical picker, following the manufacturer's instructions. Whichever method you use, careful teasing is very important if your goal is a fine, uniform woolen yarn; any small seed or fiber ball will show up in the final yarn.

After it's teased, the wool is ready to be carded with either hand cards or a drum carder. If you use hand cards as I do, you can prepare rolags or batts, depending on the type of yarn you plan to spin. Rolags are airy tubes of wool in which the fiber direction is more or less around the circumference of the tube. Batts are more like loose 'cigars' of wool in which the fibers are arranged roughly lengthwise. Whichever form you choose, the finer the yarn you plan to spin, the less wool you should load onto your cards. A common beginner's error is to put so much wool on the carding surface that it's difficult to make a light, fluffy, uniform fiber package to spin from.

Lightly load the bottom card with fiber. Begin stroking with the top card on only the lower third of the bottom card surface, progressing upward with each stroke. Transfer the wool from one card to the other, catching only the fiber *tips* which are extending *beyond* the carding surface. This will prevent the fibers from folding back on themselves and developing a lumpy "line" that will interfere with even drawing when you spin. Again, stroke the cards lightly, beginning at the base of the card and progressing upward. Just barely brush the surfaces of the card teeth together—they shouldn't mesh and drag through each other. Repeat this process as necessary, transferring the wool from one card to the other, until the wool is uniformly distributed and aligned.

Begin carding stroke on the lower third of the card surface.

Progress upward, covering two-thirds of surface with the next stroke, and then card the entire surface.

When transferring fibers from one card to the other, catch only the fiber tips into the first rows of the other card to avoid a line of folded fibers.

To remove the wool from the card, use the top edge of the empty card to loosen the fiber mass from the top edge of the loaded card. For a rolag, roll the mass of wool into a loose tube, working down the face of the card. For a batt, start at the side of the card and roll across.

If you're using a drum carder, follow the manufacturer's instructions. The batts can be divided into lengthwise strips or into crosswise sections and rolled into rolags.

Worsted Preparation. If the wool is fairly long (4″ or more), and you want a denser, less fuzzy yarn, you need to prepare it so that the natural fiber alignment is preserved from scouring through combing and spinning. To scour, place the fleece in a neat layer with the cut ends aligned in a mesh bag or screen tray. Submerge it carefully in the hot water, being careful not to disturb the locks. Some spinners find that scouring each lock of fleece separately, swishing it by hand through hot, soapy water and then through an equally hot rinse water, is worth the effort. To maintain the lock structure, hold the lock at its base and clean the tip; then reverse your grip and clean the cut end. While this sounds more time-consuming, it actually goes very quickly, and most vegetable matter is removed during the washing. After the locks are clean and dry, tease them by grasping a lock firmly at both ends and see-sawing it between your hands to open up the fibers and allow any remaining debris to drop out.

At this point, you can use a flick carder to tease and fluff the fibers while maintaining the lock configuration. Pull out a lock and hold it while popping the flicker up and down on one end. Then reverse the lock and repeat the flicking procedure on the other end. You can spin the lock as it is now, and the resulting yarn, although technically a woolen yarn, will be something between a woolen and worsted in character.

Or you can comb the locks to remove the shorter fibers. Historically, there was a variety of combing devices; many spinners today use a dog stripping comb from the pet supply store. Hold it firmly in one hand, or attach it to a solid surface, and pull each lock through the teeth. Holding the cut end of the lock, pull the tip end through the teeth, starting with the first inch and moving toward the center of the lock with each pass. Reverse the lock and repeat the process from the cut end. Short fibers will be retained in the comb; you can set these aside to card into woolen yarns, if you wish. Since a worsted yarn is spun from the cut end of the fiber, set the combed locks aside carefully with the tips all lying in one direction.

You can also comb locks with a worsted flicker or one of your hand cards. Hold the flicker in one hand while you comb a fiber lock through the coarse teeth with a flicking action from the center of the lock outward. Then reverse the lock and repeat the process on the other end. This opens up the fiber tips and removes any shorter fibers from the base.

You can spin directly from the combed locks, being careful to make sound joins in the yarn, or you can prepare a top. One way to do this is by overlapping a series of locks by half their staple length. Carefully draw this out into a thinner top, and then prepare a second one and lay them side by side. Twist them together lightly into a single top by winding them onto a spindle shaft or large knitting needle. When this is removed from the shaft,

Combing Locks With a Pet Rake

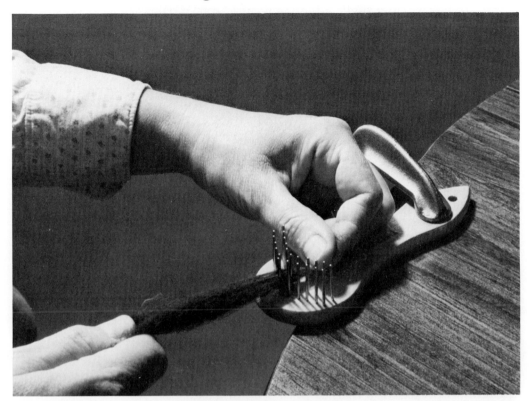

Begin combing at the tip.

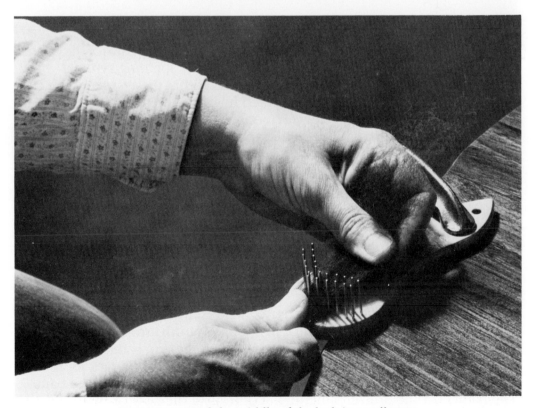

Progress toward the middle of the lock in small steps.

it's ready for spinning. Or, you can catch the tips of several locks into the comb and draw off a sliver which is wound into a ball as before.

Wool combing for a *true* worsted yarn requires special equipment, time and skill in fiber preparation. The very finest and smoothest yarns are made with combed yarns. Historically, though, wool prepared in the home was more likely to be woolen or of a worsted type such as described above. Wool combing was the work of professionals, usually men, as the tools were heavy and the job arduous. Today, with lighter tools available, many handspinners are exploring this option. To learn more about wool combing, read *Hand Wool Combing and Spinning* by Peter Teal.

Commercially Prepared Fibers. Another option to consider is prepared fibers. Small cottage industries as well as large mills are now producing carded batts, roving, and combed top for handspinning. Some specialize in identifiable sheep breeds, some in special color blending. In buying prepared fibers, you give yourself more time to spend with your spinning wheel and knitting needles. On the other hand, you lose the chance to select a specific fleece for a given project, and the gentle handling that's possible when all processing is done by hand.

Regardless of how you achieve it, your goal should be a high quality fiber preparation. A traditional knitting yarn is even both in twist and diameter, and this can't be achieved unless the fibers are drawn from a clean, light and airy fiber source. The quality of fine yarn depends on careful and thorough preparation. Poor quality yarns are more often the result of inadequate fiber preparation than of poor spinning skills!

Yarn Types

The following spinning techniques are ones I use to construct traditional-style knitting yarns. While there are only two basic spinning systems (woolen and worsted), a number of variations within these systems are possible. The yarn type definitions presented here are not standard terminology, but they do classify several variations within the two systems according to the way the fibers are aligned in the yarn.

I generally spin in the "Z" direction with a relatively low twist, then ply loosely in the "S" direction; how much twist depends on how fine the yarn. The finer the yarn, the higher the twist. The twisting action that occurs as you pass the yarn around the needle with each stitch adds a little twist to your knitting yarn as you work. If your yarn is spun in the S direction and plied Z, it will actually untwist as you knit, sometimes to the point that the yarn loses its strength. Knitting yarns of the past were usually twisted more firmly than is common today, as durability took precedence over loft and softness of hand.

I also usually spin with a "long draw"; that is, the hand with the fiber supply draws away from the orifice in a long, smooth arm-length motion, staying just ahead of the advancing twist. When the arm is fully extended and the yarn has enough twist in it to keep it from drifting apart, let the yarn feed onto the bobbin with one smooth forward motion of the hand. The hand near the orifice, rather than controlling the flow of twist, only occasionally grips the fibers so that thicker places can be drawn out. If you

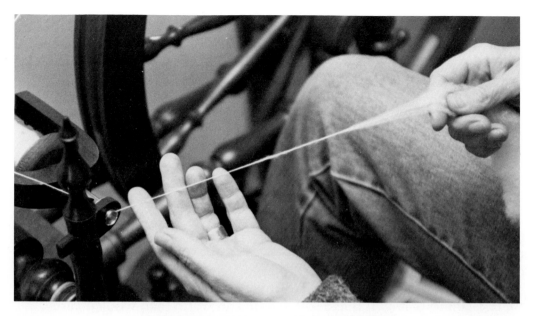

Beginning a long draw from a woolen rolag.

find the drawing out process difficult and you have to tug at the yarn, the twist is probably advancing into your fiber supply. Try slowing down your treadling and/or adjusting the belt tension so you can keep the drawing out ahead of the twist. As you work with different yarn types, you will need to vary the length of the draw to suit the yarn preparation.

True Woolen Yarn. This type is spun from a light, airy rolag prepared as described on page 168. A soft yarn requires only enough twist to hold it together; more twist will give you a firmer, more durable yarn. The more fiber you have carded into your rolag, the heavier your yarn will be. For a yarn in which the fibers are randomly arranged with much air incorporated, use the long draw, holding the rolag very lightly. This yarn style is highly elastic, especially if the wool has a fine crimp.

A garment knit of woolen yarn has extremely soft to moderately soft hand, depending on the degree of twist in the yarn. It is very warm because of the protruding fibers that trap air in the interstices of the stitches as well as within the yarn itself.

I find that a well-made woolen yarn is the best all-purpose knitting yarn. This type of yarn is suitable for very fine to bulky weights, and can use very short to medium-long fibers.

Semi-Woolen Yarn is spun from a carded batt of roughly aligned fibers rolled across the card surface into a cigar-shaped cylinder. If the wool has been carded on a drum carder, the batt is torn into strips in the direction of the fiber. Commercially prepared roving results in a similar yarn. Use a long draw while holding the fiber source lightly so as not to disturb the fiber alignment. Spun with a low twist, this fiber preparation will give a moderately soft yarn; but because the fibers are arranged roughly parallel to each other, it is slightly less elastic and lightweight than a comparable woolen yarn. With fewer fibers protruding, it is is less likely to pill. Since less air is incorporated into the yarn, it is more compact and less warm than a woolen yarn.

If spun with a fairly high twist, semi-woolen yarns are compact and heavy, able to withstand hard wear. The semi-woolen method is suitable for fine to chunky yarns, and should be made of medium to long fibers.

Worsted-Type Yarn is spun from a combed lock with all the fibers the same length and in parallel alignment. If you insert only the amount of twist necessary to hold the fibers in place and ply the yarn, it will be soft and lofty; more twist will result in a smooth, hard yarn that is extremely durable. To spin this type of yarn, use a modified long draw. Try holding further back on the lock, extending the drafting zone to accommodate the fiber length, while playing the fibers out of the combed locks carefully to maintain fiber alignment. Remember to spin from the cut end of the fiber, not the tip.

A variation on this technique is to fold a combed lock over your forefinger and spin from the middle of the fiber. Especially if you're spinning a very long wool, you'll find this method gives good control.

Worsted-type yarn is very hard wearing, smooth and compact, and therefore resistant to pilling. It is less soft, elastic and warm than woolen yarns, for little air is incorporated into it. This yarn is ideal for patterns requiring clear stitch definition, or for a garment which will receive hard wear. An exceedingly fine yarn, appropriate for open lace work, can be spun from combed locks. Very fine to bulky yarns can be made from long to extra-long fibers with this spinning technique; the heavier yarns are best constructed using several plies.

Spinning a worsted yarn from a lock folded over the index finger.

True Worsted Yarn is spun from wool that has been combed into a long, smooth, uniform 'top' with a pair of wool combs. The combing process removes every trace of shorter fibers and other irregularities, and creates a continuous length of parallel fibers which require few if any joins in spinning. When spinning, you musn't let the twist enter the drafting zone until the fibers are as parallel as possible and fully drafted. The principal difference between true worsted and worsted-type yarns is the degree of smoothness and uniformity. A relatively soft yarn that is hard wearing and pill resistant can be spun with minimal twist. With increased twist, the yarn will be hard wearing and able to maintain a clear surface, but with greatly reduced elasticity. True worsted yarns can be very fine to bulky; as in worsted-type yarns, the heavier weights are usually constructed from several plies.

Semi-Spun Yarn. This is a yarn style, relatively new in folk knitting, which can be spun from a carded batt or roving, combed locks, or combed top. As its name implies, there is little or no twist added. Semi-spun yarns are necessarily bulky weight, because their strength comes from the quantity of overlapping fibers, not from twist. This type of yarn is most easily spun on a bulk head wheel or a spindle. It can also be done on a standard flyer wheel, provided the orifice and hooks are large enough. Holding the fiber source lightly in one hand and working directly in front of the orifice, draw the fibers out while simultaneously feeding the yarn onto the bobbin, allowing very little twist to accumulate. This isn't very satisfactory, though, because most bobbins are too small to hold much of the bulky yarn and you're working against what the wheel was designed to do. You can modify a flyer wheel by wedging an improvised spindle into the orifice. A knitting needle of a size that fits the orifice, cut 6″-8″ long, works well. If you plan to spin this type of yarn (or any bulky yarn, for that matter) regularly, you'll be happier with a bulk head wheel.

Semi-spun yarn is very soft and light weight; it incorporates a lot of air because there is so little twist to confine the fibers. A garment knit of this yarn is very warm for its weight, as the yarn expands to fill in all the spaces in the knit structure because the yarn is so open. However, it isn't very wind resistant. Any elasticity in this type of yarn is a result of fiber crimp, not the spin, but the looped knit structure does give the garment some elasticity.

Semi-spun yarns knit up rapidly and can be used as a single, because skewing isn't a problem at such a low twist level. A two-ply, plied with a very low twist, will be more durable, however. Spinners sometimes construct this type of yarn from shorter fibers or from a rolag; such a yarn might be beautiful initially, but pilling and matting become serious problems with use. Extra long fibers, combed or from a batt, are most suitable for this type of yarn. If you want an unspun yarn such as Icelandic lopi, start with a combed top of 10″ long fibers and draw it out on a shaft, not a spinning wheel.

Selecting Yarn Types

No yarn is ideal in every way for its end use; each selection involves compromise. For example, to have the softness, elasticity and light weight of a woolen yarn, you must put up with some pilling and lack of durability—or else increase the durability with greater twist at the expense of a soft hand. For clearly defined stitches and the hard wearing quality of a worsted, you must be satisfied with a denser yarn with less elasticity, but a high resistance to pilling. In every case, you must weigh all factors and decide which features are most important to you, and then correlate yarn type to the fiber length of the available fleece. The accompanying chart, "Fiber Length to Yarn Type", suggests which fiber lengths are most suitable for the yarn types described here.

Selected Sheep Breed Suitable for Knitting Yarns

Fiber Fineness		
Fine, 17-22 microns	**Medium, 22-31 microns**	**Coarse, 31-36 microns**
Merino	Targhee	Romney
Rambouillet	Finnsheep	Perendale
Cormo	Corriedale	
Debouillet	Columbia	
	Dorset	
	Romeldale	

Fiber Length				
Very short, under 2″	**Short, 2″-4″**	**Medium, 3″-5″**	**Medium-long, 4″-6″**	**Long to Extra-long, 5″ and over**
Lambswool	Merino	Columbia	Cormo	Romney
	Rambouillet	Finnsheep	Corriedale	Perendale
		Dorset		
		Debouillet		
		Romeldale		
		Targhee		

Plying

Except for the semi-spun yarns described above, most knitting yarns spun in the home have been two- or three-ply. The term 'ply' (from *plie'*, folded) derives from folding a yarn in half, which causes the two parts to twist together in the opposite direction from which they were spun. The process of twisting two or more continuous lengths together in the opposite direction from which they were spun is a natural extension of this. Singles are most often spun in a "Z" direction, and then plied in the "S" direction. Plying the yarn back in the opposite direction from which it was spun releases some of the initial twist, allowing the yarn to become more lofty. The Z and S twists balance each other, eliminating the tendency of the knitted fabric to skew. Knitting with a single, unless it's very low twist, requires giving special attention to setting the twist and/or using a tighter gauge to control this skewing. Plying the yarn gives it strength for further handling, too.

To ply a uniform, stable knitting yarn, pay special attention to tensioning the two or more singles evenly as you twist them together. You might find it useful to make a template to guide the singles as you ply them; the shaker cap out of a spice jar is handy for fine yarns! Tie the singles onto the leader yarn; lace them between the fingers of one hand to tension them, and use the other hand to feed the plied yarn onto the bobbin. Keep the tensioning hand farthest away from the orifice, holding the singles slightly taut. When you've treadled enough twist into the plied yarn, pinch it off with the hand nearest the orifice and feed the yarn onto the bobbin. The cutting-off hand should move rhythmically back and forth between the orifice and the stationary hand. Remember to turn the wheel in the *opposite* direction from the way the singles were spun.

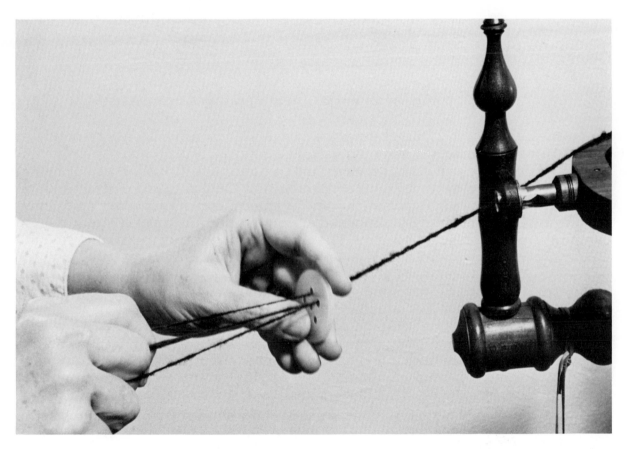

Plying with a spice jar lid as a template.

The character, strength and loft of the finished yarn is dependent on balancing the amount of twist in the single against the twist in the ply. Experiment with inserting different amounts of twist at both stages to see how this affects the final yarn.

Yarn Finish

After you've spun your yarn, you must take care to finish it properly. Before this is done, the real character of the yarn isn't necessarily evident, and determining a suitable gauge can be difficult. Finishing can soften a yarn, develop its loft, and tame some excess kinkiness. A sweater knit of unfinished yarn is likely to be heavy and lifeless because of traces of oil and dirt and unrelaxed fibers. There are several ways to finish yarn, but the goal is always to give the wool a final scouring and set the twist. ("Oiled" yarns and unspun ones are special cases and will be dealt with separately.)

The first step is to skein the yarn, loosely tying the skein in at least four places. For very fine yarns or semi-spun ones, it's a good idea to weave the ties through the skein to control tangling, and tie the skeins in six or eight places.

Weaving the ties through a skein of fine yarn helps avoid tangles.

To scour, prepare a warm water bath with enough mild, neutral detergent to make the water feel slick. Be sure to use enough water to allow the yarn to move freely. Submerge the yarn and place the pot on a medium hot burner, slowly raising the temperature to a simmer. Occasionally lift and turn the yarn, taking care to support its weight. Don't stir or agitate, as this can result in tangled skeins and felted yarn. After the water comes to a simmer, remove the pot from the heat and allow it to cool to a warm-to-the-hand temperature; drain and press the excess water from the yarn.

Add warm water, about the same temperature as the drained scouring bath, taking care that the water doesn't run directly onto the yarn. Allow it to soak until cool, and repeat this rinse soak if necessary until the rinse water is clear. At this point you can mordant and/or dye your yarn if you wish.

After rinsing, squeeze the yarn out, but don't wring the skein at any point. You can put the yarn in a pillow case and spin it dry in the washing machine. When all the excess water is out, take each skein and shake it with a vigorous snap, reverse the skein and repeat. This opens up any minor tangles that occured in the finishing bath. Next, stretch the skein between your hands and vigorously snap outward to even all the strands. Just how vigorously you handle the skeins depends on how fragile the yarn is. Hang the skeins on a rod in a well-ventilated area out of direct sunlight to dry. Knitting yarns are best dried without tension so that their loft and elasticity can develop. It's surprising how much bouncier—and shorter—the finished skein is than an unwashed one of the same yarn.

For an oiled yarn, follow the same steps, but omit the detergent and reduce the heat of the scouring bath to about 120°-130°. Enough oil will remain in the yarn to make it water repellant. Be warned, though, that an oiled yarn is not as clean, nor will it stay as clean in use, as a thoroughly scoured yarn. If too much oil is retained, it will become sticky as it oxidizes. I feel that the disadvantages that come from retaining the oils far outweigh the advantages.

An un-plied semi-spun or unspun yarn can't withstand scouring. Such a yarn must be knit first, and the whole garment scoured. Since it's the wool fibers themselves, rather than the spinning, that determines the character of this type of yarn, working with the unfinished yarn doesn't alter the final appearance of the garment. But always work up a swatch and scour it first, and plan for any necessary adjustments to the garment size that the final scouring will cause. Or carefully steam the yarn to set the twist, as described below, before you begin knitting.

Having followed the scouring process described above, your yarn should be clean, and the twist set. As you work a gauge sample, check carefully for any tendency of the swatch to lean in the direction of the twist. If there seems to be some skewing, you may want to take further steps to set the twist. My method is to set a teakettle on to boil, and when it's steaming vigorously, I pass every part of the skein through the steam about 6″-8″ above the spout while stretching it gently between my hands. Then I set it aside to cool and dry with just enough tension to hold it straight, but not stretch it. If you use this method, be careful not to burn your hands in the live steam. You can also switch to a smaller needle size and/or knit more firmly. A hard, firm gauge will often control skewing, as we can see in old folk sweaters knit from bulkier single yarns, but this does make for a heavier garment.

Your yarn is now finished and ready for the knitting needles. Unless you're going to start knitting immediately, store the yarn in skeins, not balls. Balls compress the yarn, and loft and elasticity can be lost, especially if they are wound too tightly. Besides, skeins of handspun yarns are a feast for the eyes, beautiful in themselves.

A Selected List of Suppliers

Brown Sheep Company, Inc. Route 1, Mitchell, Nebraska 69357.
single wool yarn in medium and heavy weights, single mohair-lambswool yarn, two-ply bulky yarn.

Canterbury Yarns. Corvallis, Oregon.
Imported New Zealand fisherman's wool in two-ply worsted.

Caswell Sheep & Wool Company. Route 1, Box 135, Blanch, North Carolina 27212.
Two-ply woolen yarn, 50-50 blend of Corriedale and Rambouillet.

Charity Hill Farm, Inc. Hardwick, Massachusetts 01037.
Two-ply sport and heavy weight yarns.

Indian Valley Spinner. 1910 Elm Avenue, Cincinnati, Ohio 45212.
Bulk head spinning wheel.

Janknits. Ingomar, Montana 59039.
Columbia fleece of the Mysse Ranch Company in two- and three-ply worsted and three-ply ragg. (Traditional sweater kits also available.)

Meg Swansen. 6899 Cary Bluff, Pittsville, Wisconsin 54466.
Full range of books and traditional knitting yarns, including Icelandic lopi in plates and Shetland yarns.

William Condon & Sons, Ltd. P.O. Box 129, 203 Fitzroy Street, Charlotte, Prince Edward Island, Canada C1A 7K3.
Single through five-ply worsted, and unspun yarns.

Bibliography

Abbey, Barbara. *The Complete Book of Knitting.* New York: Viking, 1971.

Alafoss of Iceland, *Reynolds Lopi.* New York: Reynold Yarns—Alafoss of Iceland, 1983.

Australian Wool Corporation. *Traditional Knitting with Wool.* Australian Wool Corp., 1982.

Bohn, Annichen Sibbern. *Norwegian Knitting Designs.* Oslo: Grondahl & Son, 1975.

Chadwick, Eileen. *The Craft of Hand Spinning.* New York: Charles Scribner's Sons, 1980.

Compton, Rae. *The Complete Book of Traditional Knitting.* New York: Charles Scribner's Sons, 1983.

Dale Yarn Company. *Knit Your Own Norwegian Sweaters.* New York: Dover Publications, 1974.

Davenport, Elsie G. *Your Handspinning.* Missouri: Select Books, 1953.

Don, Sarah. *Fair Isle Knitting.* London: Mills & Boon Ltd., 1979.

-----. *The Art of Shetland Lace.* Bell & Hyman Ltd., 1981.

Debes, Hans M. *Foroysk Bindingarmynstur.* Torshavn: Foroyskt Heimavirki, 1969.

Fanderl, Lisl. *Bauerliches Stricken.* Rosenheim: Rosenheimer, 1975.

-----. *Bauerliches Stricken 2.* Rosenheim: Rosenheimer, 1979.

-----. *Bauerliches Stricken 3.* Rosenheim: Rosenheimer, 1983.

Fee, Jacqueline. *The Sweater Workshop.* Loveland, Colorado: Interweave Press, 1983.

Gainford, Veronica. *Designs for Knitting Kilt Hose and Knickerbocker Stockings.* Edinburgh: Scottish Development Agency, 1978.

Guojonsson, Elsa E. *Notes on Knitting in Iceland.* Reykjavik: National Museum of Iceland, 1979.

Gustafson, Paula. *Salish Weaving.* Vancouver: Douglas & McIntyre Ltd., 1980.

Haglund, Ulla, and Ingrid Mesterton. *Bohus Stickning, 1939-1969.* Utgiven av Foreningen Bohus Stickning, 1980.

Hartley, Marie, and Ingilby, Joan. *The Old Hand Knitters of the Dales.* England: Dalesman, 1951.

Harvey, Michael, and Rae Compton. *Shire Album 31: Fisherman Knitting.* England: Shire Publications Ltd., 1978.

Hinchcliffe, Frances and Santina, Levey. "Glove, Cap, and Boot-Hose", *Crafts.* July/August, 1982.

Hollingworth, Shelagh. *The Complete Book of Traditional Aran Knitting.* New York: St. Martin's Press, 1982.

Johansson, Britta, and Nilsson, Kersti. *Binge—en Hallandsk Sticktradtion.* Stockholm: LTs Forljg, 1980.

Kiewe, Heinz Edgar. *The Sacred History of Knitting.* Oxford: Art Needlework Industries Limited, 1971.

Lane, Barbara. "The Cowichan Knitting Industry", *Anthropology in British Columbia,* 2:14-27. Provincial Museum, 1951.

Lind, Vibeke. *Knitting in the Nordic Tradition.* Asheville: Lark Books, 1984.

McGregor, Sheila. *The Complete Book of Traditional Fair Isle Knitting.* New York: Charles Scribner's Sons, 1982.

-----. *The Complete Book of Traditional Scandinavian Knitting.* New York: St. Martin's Press, 1984.

-----. *Traditional Knitting.* London: B.T. Batsford Ltd., 1983.

Meikle, Margaret. "The Cowichan Knitting Industry", unpublished paper presented to the Native American Art Studies Association, 1983.

Morgan, Gwyn. *Traditional Knitting Patterns of Ireland, Scotland, and England.* New York: St. Martin's Press, 1981.

Norbury, James. *Traditional Knitting Patterns.* New York: Dover Publications, 1973.

Pearson, Michael. *Traditional Knitting: Aran, Fair Isle and Fisher Ganseys.* New York: Van Nostrand Reinhold Co., 1984.

Reese, Sharron. *Jigging—100% Hand Worsted.* Cornelius: John & Helen Meck, 1984.

Ross, Mabel. *The Essentials of Handspinning.* Devon: Mabel Ross, 1980.

-----. *The Essentials of Yarn Design for Handspinners.* Devon: Mabel Ross, 1983.

Simmons, Paula. *Spinning and Weaving with Wool.* Seattle: Pacific Search Press, 1977.

Smith, Mary, and Maggie Twatt. *A Shetland Pattern Book.* Lerwick: The Shetland Times Ltd., 1979.

Teal, Peter. *Hand Woolcombing & Spinning.* Dorset: Blandford Press Ltd., 1976.

Thomas, Mary. *Mary Thomas's Knitting Book.* New York: Dover Publications, 1972.

Thomas, Mary. *Mary Thomas's Book of Knitting Patterns.* New York: Dover Publications, 1972.

Thompson, Gladys. *Patterns for Guernseys, Jerseys & Arans.* New York: Dover Publications, 1971.

Turnau, Irena. "The Knitting Crafts in Europe from the Thirteenth to the Eighteenth Century", *The Bulletin of the Needle and Bobbin Club,* Vol. 65, No. 1 & 2, 1982.

van der Klift-Tellegen, Henriëtte. *Knitting from the Netherlands.* Asheville: Lark Books, 1985.

Walker, Barbara. *Charted Knitting Designs.* New York: Charles Scribner's Sons, 1972.

Wright, Mary. "Cornish Guernseys and Knitfrocks", Alison Hodge/ *Ethnographic,* 1979.

Zimmermann, Elizabeth. *Knitting Workshop.* Pittsville, Wisconsin: Schoolhouse Press, 1981.

Index